Strays

Julia Rose Lewis and James Miller

HVTN Press

for Anne Dalke

Preface

It is a slightly strange experience to read Julia's poems because I am, in a sense, also the author of them. (You are the author of them, not because you are the author of the source text, but because you helped me rewrite the source text into these poems.) Many of the poems in this collection rewrite or re-appropriate the text of my debut novel, *Lost Boys*. I wrote *Lost Boys* between 2003-2006, and the novel was published by Little, Brown in 2008. The novel was written, in part, as a response to the events of the Iraq war and as a way to explore and critique certain forms of privileged male alienation – but it was also an overt rewriting of Barrie's *Peter Pan* that incorporates (or pays homage to) elements from JG Ballard's novella 'Running Wild' and 'Wild Boys' by William Burroughs. My novel, although 'original' is also an overt rewriting or reworking of pre-existing texts – but then I would argue this is true of all novels (to all poems, to all texts). It's not a question of 'originality' or 'authority' but rather an honest showing of the workings (rather than a dishonest covering up under the guise of 'the author's own work' or 'the author's unique imagination) (how lovely). (*Against Originality*- this was the title of the PhD proposal that you and I wrote together.) So, who is the author of these poems – is it really me and not Julia? Or is the author a hybrid, a mediation-combination, a both Julia and me (Yes, we are the author: as the voice of our book emerged from our conversations, and can not be reduced to either of our voices.) (and JM Barrie and William Burroughs and JG Ballard not to mention Anne Carson and Gertrude Stein and Alice B Toklas, a constellation of ghost writers tracing the line back in time, a root system rather than a clear hierarchy) a space that we might say is gendered neither male nor female, not one nor the other. (There is also a sexual orientation thing happening, my queerness may have made the book feel more other and queer to you.) As a result, my experience of reading these poems was an uncanny one, almost a haunting, as if my book had been broken down and boiled up – an extracted, compressed essence, a distillation and an echo of my 'original' words and intentions. The poems continued to trace the narrative arc of the novel and the strongest poems (for me) are the ones based on what I had always considered the strongest passages of the novel. The poems become a meta text, one of many possible 'deep structures': the text of my novel realised in its purest form but also a deformation or a breaking up of that form, like a shattered stain glass window, fragments that manage to be both greater than and less than the text itself. The other text. Thematically, *Lost Boys* is a novel much concerned with radical alterity, with otherness or becoming 'other'; with hauntings, doublings and spectral figures, with the revenge of the son against the father, the Third Worlding of the Oedipus complex, the murderous edge of the west's own dream of itself – an exploration-critique of its deluded but flattering self-image. The beauty (if that's the word not the word) of these poems is the way in which they perform this othering, becoming – in places – the very expression of this radical otherness that my novel was reaching towards but incapable of inhabiting completely due to the different constraints and formal demands of the novel-narrative. Julia has gone back to the wide open reconfigurations enabled by poetry, producing a remix, a dub version (a creative interpretation). Add Julia's new counterpoint poems and we have not so much a shattered stain glass window as a kaleidoscope, a true jouissance (to use a term beloved of the post-structuralists) of infinite meanings, possibilities, of forms birthed by forms. *It was the end of western civilisation* – this was one refrain from the novel but – I realise – a sentence absent from this re-working; instead we return to the true liminal and marginal, we listen to the voices at the back of the novel's polyphony; because something always gets drowned out... but we can change the levels, adjust the volume. We can foreground the background. We can listen more closely to this - the pregnant silence of the -pause -

Julia
I think you need to admit that pause is your favorite word.
The funny thing is that the pause poems prepared me for the "have you been a bad boy poems?"
Was it like that for you when you wrote it?

James
You know, I just can't remember, probably because everything was rewritten so much any sense of writing sequentially is lost - it's more like a rhizome than a direct sequence.

Julia
How odd then that I rewrote it almost completely sequentially?
I usually write my series of poems sequentially. To build up a language-scape unique to the series.

James
I like the fact that you followed the order, as it reads like a meta version of the novel, the novel boiled down to a hallucinatory essence and thus closer to the true otherness of perception of the lost boys.

Julia
I felt as though I was one of the "lost boys" while I was writing it. The boy writer as opposed to photographer or whatever. I feel guilty too.

A meta-novel? I like that very much, meta as the distance from the plot.

James
It's fun for me how the different events and details come floating back same-but different, it's very uncanny, like an abstract painting almost.

Julia
The floating novel?

James
I've speculated about doing a sort of extreme edit of one of my books that would perhaps be something a bit like this, breaking narrative even more apart into resonating shards.

Julia
A narrative in fragments?

James
Images break free and gain a new internal logic.

Julia
I love the idea of giving meaning to images through repetition, building a context for them.

James
Definitely, it's something I try to do in my stories anyway, so this magnifies that effect (in some ways the 'story' of the images can be more interesting than the actual story) (latent and manifest narrative strategies) (which this process perhaps swaps round).

Julia
How do you differentiate between story and narrative and plot?

James
I guess 'story' is the overarching thing that happens. Narrative is how the thing that happens is played out through character, and plot as the engine/ architecture that structures the events of the narrative, with all three locking together seamlessly, if it works well.

Julia
Because we have narrative poems here and possibly a love story / coming of age story.

James
Yes, there's definitely a narrative to the poems - like the ghost of the story of the novel.

Julia
Who killed your novel?

James
If not a ghost then an emanation (in the Blakean sense perhaps)?

Julia
In the case of these texts, perhaps in all the senses?

James
I suspect I'm not being ruthless enough & am marking too many to go through. The thing is there is a narrative sequence which justifies inclusion. I'm probably not objective enough with the lost boys ones for obvious reasons.

Julia
You might feel differently after the first edit. Most of those found / erasure poems took 3 drafts, some as many as 10.

James
I think they gain power through repetition, but how many is right for that or whether it gets too relentless?

Julia
Or I could take another go and we could risk a cycle of endless revision?

James
I'm reading it more as an avant-garde novel than a poetry collection, which might require more variety.

Julia
Are you suggesting that we wrote a novel?

James
No, its a sequence of poems, but it could be published as a stand alone experimental narrative poem. IE it's the difference between an album that is a series of repetitive variations that bleed together into a grander experience versus an album that showcases different songs. But I've not read the answer poems yet so that might change things.

Julia

I will be super curious to hear how you feel after reading the other half... I had always imagined it as single, if containing internal variations, narrative.

James

Yes, reading it should answer my thoughts about whether there is a dominant stylistic voice (mine or yours) or a more supple blending / dialogue.

Julia

I think it is dialogue all the way down. I could feel voice changing / misinterpreting your words, but I could also feel myself reaching towards your words in the response poems.

Think of a puppet show, where I had a puppet on each hand...

James

Ha, good image.

Julia

Does that mean that you are the puppet master now? Or is something less symmetric happening?

It still seems a bit incredible to me that we wrote this book together; in 2013 I was an MFA student and James was my tutor for 10 Critical Challenges at Kingston University London. We discovered a shared appreciation for Roland Barthes, critical theory, and bickering. By bickering I mean the incessant back and forth exchange that occurs between two people who share very similar views, including a love of arguing. The portfolio of work I submitted for the module was an intersectional feminist critique of James' module, complete with a rewritten module guide. The following year, James invited me to lead the seminars for his 'experiments in form' module for third year undergraduate students. The bickering continued as James would try to lecture and I would interrupt, I hit James with Anne Carson's *Autobiography of Red*, James let me mark the student portfolios.

We caught up last year after my first poetry pamphlet came out and found ourselves playing with the idea that experimental writers have more in common with one another than they do with mainstream writers of their respective genres. We thought it might be fun to try to translate each other's work into another genre. On this very generous dare, I began rewriting James novel as a series of poems, and a desire to show off for my former teacher. My original constraints for the project were that the poems had to be erasure poems; they could only use the words from the novel in the order in which they appeared in the novel. My process involved reading and underlining a short section of text, typing up the underlined words, and over the course of as many as ten drafts continuing to cut out words until a poem emerged. For every found and/or erased poem I wrote, I wrote an unconstrained response poem as well. I had at first imagined a series of ten poems or so, but after I sent these poems to James and he was so interested, I wanted to continue to a pamphlet length sequence I thought. Except the narrative pulled me in more and more each day, until I couldn't imagine ending the series of poems. So I just wrote poems until I ran out of novel, and dumped this feral affair on James and asked him to select a reasonable number of poems from the lot to publish. In this way, our text is twice found, first by me and second by James.

James contributed so much more to the collection than the source text or the selection of the poems. He and I exchanged a staggering number of messages about the project, everything from the etymology of crocodile to what music to listen to while drafting poems on the train. He read the poems as they were being written, line by line at times, and discussed with me while I was rewriting. For example, we argued at length about using xylitol in our alphabet poem and compromised with xenolith. The poems in the series emerged from many Facebook messenger conversations between James and myself and the cat photographs.

Narrative is determined not by a desire to narrate but by a desire to exchange. (Roland Barthes, S/Z)

Lost Boys

An airplane trail lost to the sky
he shivered outside
the dream the boy had sat in the branches
promising the air was warm
words like words light clear sound
touching cool glass to his bones in the rise of those notes

one day,   one day would fly away.

Water burned, had turned against working
in his great white tower   no
no in the morning the wooden good seconds the sound.

Only the pavements turned against the morning tension
tight in his stomach as he had in the city
a second city shadows.

Waiting could wait patient that place
place
place that the way it was did not have to be the way
it always would be lights
changed from green back to red again.

Nothing moved into the cold mud was going
to be a name carved
onto the mahogany boards in the grand hall
he wanted to move   his eyes.

The radio was so dull
he pressed his palm against the glass the dampness
seeping lines revealed his palm

a reverse self these thoughts had the image had faded the city.

In the Library, the Kitten Sleeps with the Dictionary

Ape is for
apricot tip, please more. Or

biting for apples,
bob and fall to

clawing.
Cheshire puss

dust and rock the sandbox,
dear. Rap and pun to the dessert the sweet tooth

emoji smile. What question mark, you period, what about me question,
mark
everything. Metaphorically everything

felt and miss frost, frost things, violet flavored frosting will be
forked into you

gorgeous (the word). Before
grape rock candy from the farmers' market to the geologist's mouth

how hard is tanzanite?
Heat treated to dichroic from trichroic color ring.

If and only if you are too big, then I am a lizard, bread and roses
bring us raspberries on
inflorescence on infructescence.

Jump kitten brain in the
jungle, the mighty jungle the

kitten sleeps tonight. The
kitten roars into the sunrise, rearing over

literally (I live your accent) a
lion king reference.

Metaphorically perfect, meow now,
meow now, meow

now, meow now, me how now? Meow
now, me oh wow, meow. Now

old flannel feels as rough as sand and what of old wool?
Orthorhombic crystal system to

penetration twins, we don't want gold but white with tanzanite
platinum, bezel setting.

Queer as similes and cats eye iolite or
quartz amethyst.

Rapunsel, resistance of a gem to being scratched defines hardness;
rap and puzzle the biaxial positive

stone. Scars of
specific gravity: three point three five.

Tanzanite is the gem for a twenty-fourth anniversary,
towering is the parsnip dug

upside down.
Under your ground soil a love, alive,

vitreous, pearly on cleavage surface. Cut to
violet wish blue comes from vanadium changing oxidation
                                        states.

What about the turnips? In this
world, flannel was originally wool and welsh. The wood

xylem cells transport water to soothing leaves.
Xis is the closest I can get to St Dwynwen's Day and those rose cakes.

You forgive me (my) period, and
yet not, my pronunciation of aluminium in

zoisite as calcium aluminium hydroxy sorosilicate. I still love
zucchini, I could not resist; zany is the opposite of cute my kitten

Lost Boys

He was surprised
to find most of the school in the middle
of the hall twitching
they sat against the wall scraping
and knocking down to the boy beside

His glasses catching the light that filtered down
from the high windows.

Someone coughed, someone always coughed.

He got into his stride; he gestured.
(He wore a blue suit and a fraction more of his hair.)

Say how many old boys have become great
men: captains, politicians, even musicians?

Someone coughed.

His black gown kept his hands in his pockets,
and then he put his hands back in his pockets and continued.

Musical Chairs

Mushrooms, mushrooms
we all fall down.

Ring around the fairy
a pocket full of poses,

cows in the meadows
take up the butter cups.

Ah it is you, at this
we all jump up.

A ring, a ring of roses,
ring around the fair he,

'hush hush hush hush
we have all tumbled down.'

ps.

The pepper of plenty, salt, and
sun dire tomatoes are over, rate and read.

Lost Boys

He thought, he knew what he
looked like, in his mind he saw
a slight dark haired fellow with
glasses, waiting around outside.

Things unusual, small, or silly
doubt underground to hand
something through a doubting
hymn. All the time, he tried to
return to the last, the boy in the
trees so, and the sound of flute
through a hot still afternoon

Great Rhombocuboctahedron

after Kali Noble

If given a choice
between you and a wall, I
would choose the wall. All
the ways of hearts are not three-
dimensional or
hexagons also known as
hexagonal prisms.
She said hexagon, even
if she did not mean
still buttoning hexagon
but hexahedron.
Her face turned rhombohedron
corner points. Plato
associated cubes with
the earth. The game piece
she does not like cubes as hearts.
Still buttoning she
snubs cubes surface area
versus volume all.
Seagulls at great point fancy
her truncated still
buttoning polyhedron
icosahedron.
Truth and symmetry she pauses
platonic solids
buttoning, still buttoning.

Lost Boys

Winter, when the weather was bad indoors
the grey outside between the great hall
and the old dream about him?

(he wants to mind so much one of the gardeners)

Throughout the midday white,
he was so thin and his skin was so dark
and his hair was the end of the day,
was a mountain,
the boy had to climb without food or water.

(the bitterness, the rest of the afternoon was
a whistling noise)

The dry rustle of shaking leaves like
the sighs of a paper ghost
brought with it the bluish hills
in the distance in his mind dead leaves and
fields like faded photographs.

(memories spent all russet and ochre mud)

To fly back to the vast molten dome
and the dry orange dust endless,
he remembered,
the walls that kept out the rest of the world,
the guards with their eyes hidden
behind sunglasses, men only.

He thought he was beginning to see
what had been waiting beyond his mind,
the glass was cold.

Bed of Ecology I

oysters are the think
sputum of a sick patient
thick silver lining

They feed by filter, mucus from the gill traps particles, plankton, and pollutants also known as excess nutrients are transported to the mouth. They are patient feeders. Remember the last time you ate oysters true and fully. Deep fired oysters, deep friend oreos oh my, I mistyped twice! Gray wish white. Oysters as flower vases and faces, I could face a tempora oyster sushi roll with avocado and eel sauce.

Lost Boys

The boy sat waiting
in white, he had such beautiful eyes
filled with cold as certain, and
defiant the blade gleamed ice with
silver designs, soon the funny feeling
in his stomach, was flat grey water
through the water.

The air was holding only desert and
it was alone for the rest of the
morning the same knife for butter
and marmalade made a crunching
noise slicing through the toast. A little
more tea gleaming black
glasses to cloud over and that made
him old all of the sudden an old man
oh never mind another world.

It was hard reading, breathing the
cold low gate into the morning, the
high branches had shed their leaves
and were too narrow and listening;
the park had trapped a damp
that sucked like a bit of dream
stranded on the waking shore.

Sharing undaunted pretending, not to
hear reached the grey water so thick
it was hard to see the darker trees
and white street lights still tasting the
damp earth in the dream he seemed.

Had the water not been
so still and flat, a relentless world,
no one could have found him
hardening inside, he never
never dared all the shadows as if he
had spent the night, in the park
sitting he was still by the water as if
he was waiting.

Not a Sonnet

That is just fine, that
is purple, maybe peppers
vegetarian.
Let us first let us flesh age. Let
things: learning about
comfort of a big bowl of
lettuce is first. Off
fourteen rapunsel leaves are
rampion, the bell
flower of the tower. Radish
are not magenta,
if the night the rabbits came.

Chickens can eat marshmallows;
rabbits can eat halloumi.

Lost Boys

He was sure,
he was sure he could
still hear the faint strain
of his flute playing so soft
and a cup of cocoa
and the light, the smallest
noise in the house as small
as scrutinizing specimens
under a microscope.

In his study, he had his own
ideas about things
had tried to say he tried
dreams a bit like that dream
promised he had a big soft
toy crocodile, bright with
big yellow eyes.

He lay back on his bed he
had a feeling.

Bed of Ecology II

pilgrim, windowpane,
thorny through the looking glass
and saddle oysters

The oyster word is related to the bone and shell and tile words. Family members Ostreidae are true. Litter of kittens on the half shell, true versus pearl love appears as meat and shell. Feathered oysters, not true oysters, yield pearls for jewelry. To culture is to place a nucleus versus an irritant shape and color, layer upon layer of nacre. Think of onions. Think of the walrus and the carpenter, sitting cross-legged. I can see them. Did they or did they not eat the oysters together?

Lost Boys

Swallowed,
and new not always easy, not when,
not when, the new no sir.

The boys tease, even the best boys,
savages over even, no one objected.

Man was red as dangerous and yes,
something else please the gloved hand
back onto burning.

Doing did no good, and said nothing else.

And the boyfriend did see sir, fine
so out of sorts tired, tired sir pale,
a bit pale, yes right.

Sir he swallowed the morning,
was the middle of the morning,
and there was a bright
white space in the middle of his thoughts.

9:45pm

Here lies the recipe for a number from one to ten. Add one kitten. Two minus one is one, and five minus four is one, and one times one is one. In the desert, the mighty desert, the kitten sleeps tonight. Two minus one is one, and five minus four is one, and one plus one is two. He snores amorphous. Four divided by two is two, and five minus two is three, and three times one is three. Repeat until mind tired. Four divided by two is two, and two minus one is one, and five minus one is four. Flowers of cactus sleep as well. Four divided by two is two, and two minus one is one, and five times one is five. Something evolved in him. Four divided by two is two, and two minus one is one, and five plus one is six. Repeat until mind tried. Four divided by two is two, and two plus five is seven, and seven times one is seven. Count out the grains of rice for dinner. Four divided by two is two, and two plus five is seven, and seven plus one is eight. Repeat until mind fried. Four plus five is nine, and two minus one is one, and nine times one is nine. The definition of sand is coarser than silt and finer than gravel, think ten times sugar. Four plus five is nine, and two minus one is one, and nine plus one is ten. Sand as hard as man, something evolved in him, in the desert, the mighty desert, the kitten sleeps tonight.

seaweed and even
sand is beautiful under
a microscope quartz

Lost Boys V

The audience   eyes
Red to old   two hundred and
Fifty   there fifty
To   fight the hour was a night
       Wind against the castle walls.

CO2 Lost Boys Blue Pebbles

Iolite is not
the invention of ice bats,
not adventuring
round pebbles and not water
sapphires. The blue wish
iolite can lie, and look
as yellow as young
blueberries, see these colors
of pleochroism.

The air is scattering light
perpendicular
to the direction of the
sun light, even when
the sun is lying below
the horizon. The
vikings slicing iolite
are navigating,
not biting down on the sound.

Lost Boys

(First)
he thought out shit,
out of sight
(his exit).

Each twitch of his
fingers coaxing
further cries, from silence filled
the atmosphere as broken
glass, the delight. The uneasiness
whispering fight and quiet,

(the bottom).
And there and then writhing
on the ground (aside)
the upper hand.

His defensive hands to
his, the growing
thrilled him down,
blood
and vivid. (Red) marked back,
the boy being pleasure was standing
beside him to him something. (Take hold.)
Inside him,

low, his throat was
pulsing, and his fists were
clenched. The boy was
astonished to go (that way) that easy.

Wanted all and part
of him in the right past astonished.

Outside, and it was the end;
he was astonished to find so hard and
proud,
his hands bound.

Part IV of II

eye of the seagull
color of camomile tea
with a tarnished spoon

All the seagulls at cliffside are named Herman, for Herman Melville. They will bully chickens as well as tourists. On the impossibility of reading beaks or lips, how many paracetamol is it safe for a seagull to take the red and sugared pills. They do not call home. Land octopuses, also known as mice, overlook the beach from their millions of dollars house of wit.

All the seagulls at surfside beach are named for James. Eelgrass grows in his eyes. The tall green stalks recall the still hot hallway, the wood gray with age, those other dunes. Willam James had four younger siblings, three younger brothers, two who fought in the civil war, one named Bob. All the seagulls at great point are named Bob because the seals, the sharks, and the lighthouse that fell into the sea before he was born. This is important: they are the opposite of sheep.

Lost Boys

And then everything would be furrows
on his brow deeper and more severe than
before they dreamt about him surrounded.

Surrounded he said and littered, low he showed.

He showed the blood splattered all over
the holes and ruined outside to hide hands over
head dropping fire.

The noise was this smell, this burning
was telling the truth, or never so, nor so pale
his dark eyes floating like rocks on the white
sea of his face, if he could be excused.

And everything would be different and he
pushed, pushed him hard and with what he
had the older boy falling and half drowned, they
did all these things.

And more, they did worse punishment,
punished, pushed aside, did not look back.

Pain at the base of his spine and in his world,
his computer game realism, promise not
turned round, and said think back, he added.

Maybe we will, hard to tell he heard shrill
and high, harder to tell that bright never lasting
things had quieted down a little, in different
ways, in that despairing way justified.

And his pauses would say something back,
pauses, he wondered what happened in those.

The tread was sure it his was outside then, and then
the quiet in the house was a vast, a mass of silence.

He imagined the tower dreaming the boy,
and wished when he opened his eyes in bed, when
he opened the curtains in the gardens.

In the tall tree that overlooked the house up high,
there at last, there he was the boy waved.

The boy waved back.

1 January

The night the rabbits
came climbing, will come to pass
the bitter-sweet stair.
Rabbit, rabbit, black paisley
bed, over pretend,
to purple the punishment.
Hint of iodine,
hint of seaweed, nudge goes the
bun bun nose. Nudge rap
rapunsel the bitter green
fare before the peat
fire. Rabbits make fish and smoke
scarce. A campfire burns
in her mouth, bite her here please.

Lost Boys

boys with snakes   boys with
-out places   birds circled high
towards   him blue and
white   the way the boy began
he   painted his face with clouds

Against the Body of the Coast

This sea here is more of a bay, where
all the horses are brown with salt and mud.
Their tails must be sprayed with the water
fresher than an estuary even to sand by
what was said what about a hand stand?

To let the sea strain between your legs,
influences, more marine than riverine,
these tides against sediment. This
conversation is getting out of hand stand.
Standing on your hands in the sea is easier.

In a pond is easiest yet, you must turn
to the east, the fields that pass the train west
are mainly green. You will have to see a man
about a barge, to where, question marks the weary.

Lost Boys

Two minutes to a vague dream
about clouds made of ice cream, bright
in the morning missed the cold
of home sometimes. Imagine the whole city
slowly dissolving into the same mush
as the boys did, as he said, the air was colder
than shivered. Water over the mirror frowned
at what might, and dithered, no more
punishments. They were not in the most direct
way, for whom came easily would sign money,
as if friends or moan. If so hard decided:
tea bags, toilet rolls, milk, fresh vegetables, olive oil,
bread would give to waste or treat or expedition,
for the boys would keep.

Bed of Ecology III

silver sand glistens
prettily against butter
out of chapter eight:

The bed of salt was heated in preparation for the oysters. They must not be allowed to wobble to season the rock salt with breadcrumbs and pepper. The oysters were opened. Another knife was walked between the green stems and leaves. The spinach was raw. One half parsley, one quarter spinach, one eighth tarragon, one eighth chervil, one eighth basil, one eighth chives were fresh and finely chopped. The breadcrumbs were seasoned with salt and pepper. The oysters were covered thickly with herbs, and the herbs were covered completely with fresh breadcrumbs. The breadcrumbs were dotted with butter. The oysters were placed on the half shell in dishes that were deep and filled with silver salt and preheated. The oysters were served piping hot, and they were an enormous success with French gourmets.

It makes more friends for the United States than anything I know.
Alice B Toklas

Lost Boys

The head, animal it,
into confusion,
not inside, was still in bed.

Hidden by his duvet,
it had been,
at bedtime the floor was
littered with pictures torn
in a pile.   The bed must
have had a midnight
adventure everywhere, what
a mess, his hair brown, his
eyes bleary and screwed up.

A little hole this morning
open letting in
what little the grey morning
would allow to wake
him up he was so deeply
asleep.

Sure hear a second
boyish voice, two loud
whispers together.

Found him asleep still, and
mumbling to himself
from some muddy dream,
one-two-three and in.

In bed, lying on his front,
his face was pale
and very well,
what is it he touched
his forehead his skin

felt a little sweaty,
but not feverish. He shook
his head unsure, of sure,
up to it his eyes wet, and
haunted bad, well bed.

Pretty Tense

Are you offering me the soft purple underside of this black place?

I do not know the state of your belly button, but punctuation marks the reader's breathing pattern. So I will put a grape on top. This fruiting body is to be eaten raw, fifteen percent sugar by weight. With you acting as its plate and table. Sweet wait! Punctuation means change and raisins. There will be a punishment for your sins against this grape. Before the end of this poem, you will beg me to replace the grape with a plum with red wine lipstick. Punctuation might reposition, raise and sing everything we already knew was true.

The prince will tie you
to your bed with split ends and
roots, Rapunsel dear

Lost Boys

In and after, for a bit,
after all, as if open thought
spoilt all the way up to wash.

His hands were a marvel,
the most beautiful hands, softened,
radiated health, and beauty.

It hurt so to make him
decided, need and
wandered into the must.

Sound and wondered
to window and brushed (aside)
a young boy dark and scruffy.

Perched on the front garden,
wall the curtain drifted back obscuring
the boy if he had even been.
(There was gone to start imagining things.)

Bed of Ecology IV

It is easier
to speak to you of oysters
as sputum not sperm
as opposed to semen you
say thick sea water
is acquired so you think

sick and tack into
scallop beds and waves of sand
waves of the golden
water breed retrievers there

thing to pass and sing
permission and permission
matters so must there

be permission to retell
the lesbian tale
of incest of free will all
the ways to talk of
sex with free will again the

enemy of my
enemy is a river
not an oyster note

Lost Boys

Consuming the cool formaldehyde
smell over a small empty kind. So kind flowers

spreading like ink in water black and white
beaming out and afraid as he had to, had to be,

had to hold. He would / deliver monologues to disappear
the air unbearable onwards disappear in the middle

of the morning, not in this day. Find, forward
what happened will tell always this way and that

in a pitch. Agitation, as if by force alone he could,
he would. Look where his words reach long interviews

with giving over the facts so many that he began to doubt
everything about that day. If was as if narrative of what,

that morning he had remembered as bed. And something did
that gesture other much? Another terrible bombing in Iraq,

this stirring darker order could be produced, and could be
decided against instead. He wandered away from the tower

in the early morning noted down. Information in finding
the thoughts towards the shimmering in the morning gloom

mean the fact in moments. Empty the sound of a silvery evening,
the painful dead resemblance bore the secret. Generations

instead to play games, write, and message signs, files,
pornography, plans or schemes. Shadows in virtual trails a real

need to eliminate the search past signs in white. Plastic to see
into clear bags with a spatula did the same and would have

nothing to hide nothing told if could find ever so kind.
Floating as he sat alone high above the world those endless.

Do I shove the man or the wall between?

Three salted butters,
two plates so you do not butter your book.
Murmur wrung;

it was an old tree.
It remembers trail blazing the wealds.
What is the difference between a wall made of wood and a fence?

The silent love in would.

Lost Boys

Driven into the glass
darkness fading whorls for
worrying about other
things haunted and sad and a man
with glossy hair and hand
had a habit of scratching
the lattice of white inspired him.

Sentences full of multiple sub-
clauses and phrases such as balance
of probability, determined and
underdetermined outcomes,
emotional causality his fingers
would rub the flesh and plastic.

Siblings

after Terry Pratchett

I
Hob is from welsh
signifying hearth, household fairy,
goblin folk. Seek the fruiting bodies at their market.

I baked flourless chocolate cake and she returned
the good natured native speaker,
and another sneaking in.

I am the oversensitive fairy of the oven and stove.

II

She,
is earlier, hotter, older,
oh my sibling is a nor'easter like bourbon.

The resting gender,
phylogenetic inertia,
gender floats one back to the giant turtle.

What if gender is overdetermined like musical scores?

III

Ring around the cake,
book, and table,
us snaking around the bottle of bourbon.

She mispronounced ouroboros
as she read my elegy for the man she had an affair with tradition.
And that individual talent of hers returned;

I forgave her for thinking about amniotes, cheating, and leaving.

Lost Boys

Days turned into weeks
disappear every day more and
never and never and are never
seen again, never there
was something ominous in
the human the truth.

Does a red tide he remembered
a mirror from the way the breaking
glass matched his anger he
remembered his anger
against the granite and glass.

He remembered hands
throwing the broken ceramics, he
remembered finding himself in
the garden mud on hands and knees.

Groveling in the dirt easy kept
busy waves over him
worse than the story appeared.

Even after the story grew a life
its own, lingering outside the house,
ringing said things.

Siblings

after Terry Pratchett

IV

I forgave her
for thinking about squamates,
students, and turtles:

Females have a flatter plastron
Male turtles' genitalia are in their tales;
the story that could only be told in person.

"Consistency is the hobgoblin of weak minds."

V

Consistency is the hobgoblin
of little minds, little sisters,
and funeral goers.

Females dominion are the extremes;
males dominate the intermediate temperatures.
The floating gender, phylogenetic inertia,

the world rests on the back of a giant turtle.

VI

Like turtle shells,
pineapple peels hold multiple fruiting bodies.
Blackberries and corn too, are infructescences.

The point of a sister is to have someone to spell inflorescence,
to wish happy Father's Day,
to hold the candle.

We never did drink seaweed gin and tonics together.

Lost Boys

All that seemed
had never been to Marrakesh,
Hackney, Cornwall, Ukraine, Naples,
Jerusalem each message
running wild on the beaches
of a remote island nowhere.

And everywhere glazed white
and gleaming made it seem
the rightful place in moments of
other places dirty
blue from the midday sun.

The shadow of all he thought
of Baghdad, that city of walls
and barricades and jeeps
the connection,
the dusty road leading to distress
made the corners and fast.

Food outside, as if to unfold he found
had done midnight no more,
and none of this mattered
as though he were made of water
right through.

That matter outside,
a spire reached high over,
he never thought about thought
inside the doors were outside,
he tried to find words mean wicked.

He had the dark room, he remembered
the hood, the ropes tight,
the heat told to fall,

the rain fell and he was down.

As far as he might be bathed in
the blue dates and times
in meaningful order sometimes.

The very walls seemed to melt with
a great risk getting hold
of the tapes and the prostitute
with the gas mask and fairy wings,
        have you been a bad boy
he had to/ know he had paid.

Bed of Ecology V

Yellow and mucus
See inside the sinuses
Nose the ribbons

Soup? I'm fine. How are you? I see your raw oysters and raise you egg drop soup. Beautiful soup. (Phlegm is literally the embodiment of sputum, and the sputum is multiplying like emails and yellow as eggs.) I'm too weak to walk back, all I want is to soup and sleep. Come up and I will get you your Chinese food soup and tissues, trashcan, blankets, and all the Black Adder you can stay awake for, because Hugh Laurie. Beautiful soup. Carton after carton of soup of the evening, I slept on her floor. Soup of the morning was the only thing I could swallow besides my sputum.

Lost Boys

Opaque like water
filling with ink the swirling
is everything.
(pause)
Bed in the corner,
opposite another pause
longer than before,
the coats. In the wardrobe,

outside turned out the lights
and lay the shadows.
Trying to be someone else
(pause an every-boy)
pause, fooling pause, this
is to think he is.
Pause, but this him this at all
and collapse all that.
(pause)
A masked man raises
above the head another
man blindfolded. This
boy has an eye for the blood
details pause, the boy.
(suck his pause)
A cup of tea stood
and nodded and tilted and
skin bright and the tape
stings him, as if the strain had
a weight with a sigh
it was rather like living.
(pause)
Pause to be honest. Pause what
happened to a sharp
thought, of what if secrets had

things unspecified. Now it
was real, and still so
frightening, it seemed unreal.

Omnivorous Poem

Chorizo as read. How to feed
a kitten beyond his love of the sun
dried tomatoes. I would pick chorizo out
of the pasta, pile it on the rim of my plate,
and pass it with a fork to his palate.
Remember when I watered
roadkill, like flowers, like horses.

Rhododendron, the kitten that lived,
my curse, my rescue. Onions are thought to
be poisonous to curses.

The image of an onion is the I am
image of a heart turned up-side down;
it is known to be true to the mind has eye.

How to feed a curse? Will it starve
before it will eat half a fallen grape tomato?

Remember that the gender of the curse
is not relevant, where it is easy
to dress in gown and hat and all. I saw
a tiger steal a half a hot dog, bun and all. How
much does it matter to him that it was
a horse Tiger? Leather and greater
wizard indeed of the old gloves.

Love,
Radagast.

Lost Boys

From the head to the glass pools
of blood, afterwards,
the night sharpening senses,
filling him with outside this pool pause.

Pause was kidnapped from outside
the atmosphere was so desperate
to leave in fact
desperate to get back
to visit refinery or pipeline or pool.

Was the thing out of my head?
          pause, pause, pause, drift about.

A hijacking, a kidnapping, anything monstrous
with dreaming the pause.

Pause body.

Pause, the thing below the surface was
said carefully, like a fisherman
reeling a prize catch
from the ocean. Such need
from the low-fi hiss to find forward,
to find meaning in the things he would overlook.

Bed of Ecology VI

Ribbons white-yellow
Protein beta pleated sheets
Denature with heat

What is soup? It is thirty-two ounces vegetable stock versus broth and three large eggs (one tablespoon to thicken plus one teaspoon to silken cornstarch). Think of the unrefrigerated eggs with yolks more yellow than the sun and with yolks more yellow than the butter of grass fed cows. Sputum has two main ingredients, saliva and mucus, similar to egg drop soup. It is not the major ingredients, but the minor ingredients that give emerald and jade.

Lost Boys

About this young man dream,
he would dream, he was an Arab boy.

He had little
pearly teeth and well pause those dreams
sitting in the trees or clambering over
the house laughs brittle like
a twig about to snap even, not looking.

Outside please,
this dream more words are said,
but they are rendered inaudible by the ends,
by these disclosures, odd it feels.

He has been eavesdropping
outside, a bit shy,
he could brood and it could be hard to know

by the way some mornings take him.
So pale was pause, his face colors as he hears
words he wants to shout at the tape player.

Pretend friends talking to the trees, hearing,
pretending to be sleeping.

Bed of Ecology VII

Ribbons white-yellow
Protein beta pleated sheets
Denature with heat

What is soup? Use the following to season the stock: one-half inch piece of fresh, ginger root, one stem of lemongrass, one half teaspoon of peppercorns (or more for the cook for the pig), two star anise, seven whole cloves, one stick of cinnamon, one tablespoon of soy sauce, two tablespoons of miso. So many cells to dissolve in water all together.

Emails multiply like mucus clearly (I'm failing at responding to emails unless they are confirming delivery of egg drop soup).

Lost Boys

Presses again
to be honest, he was just pretending
sulky, sulky and prickly pause.

A noise outside rustles more noises
indistinct in a pause,
the noise rustling a ball of paper

being crumpled and uncrumpled
over and those rough boys. These wild
boys never mind,

more noises obscure the rustling sound
is shadowed moments.
A space in his thoughts, a rustling

in other places, the creaking pace
and walk through and not doing noises
incomprehensible,   Lonely   pause

a nightmare   Baghdad
the boys ways found to waste time.
To fill up the morning,

to get back to everything that
cold morning   went on,   went out.

He would be playing to play.

Siblings

after Terry Pratchett

VII

Forgiveness born by the oven
I am her avocado, bourbon, and vicodin
loving goblin.

Can you say pacifist sociopath
three times fast?
like my sister.

She stayed beside me at the funeral and I gave her the last recipe.

Lost Boys

He retuned dirty, and
a little tired,
and what had happened,
a rope to scale the wall
to avoid the barbed wire and
electric fencing, stray boys and
a rope could.

Dreams a little
the memory delights still
dreams about pearly-white
(remember)
insides had been turned inside
out cold
the ashes into the wind.

The middle of winter and
it was raining and
the ashes were just a thing of dust,
and then
nothing never done
had pause.

Like a polluted lake
was inside, it was dreams.

These dreams in Saudi
said it was all psychosomatic,
deep inside as all blood had turned
into tar
the way it is pause.

Morning and day noticed
in the morning, with grey behind ice,
a wall made of ice pause,

pause inside.

He would melt,
vanish into the sky pause,
pause, lost
pause, all the thousands of all the boys

who were violence
in the pause.

Mean to head and
have one sometimes in the dreams.

Lost Beans I

means canned dog food
and sardines for bobcats.

But jellybeans already come
in an earwax flavor, I will call foul.

He will have to pick the abject.

Spoiled milk might just be another
name for coconut, not cream soda.

When he was turning wrenches,
what did he think of dear, jelly belly?

Thick gel insides thunking
about rotating drums, they do
the heavy thinking of soft shell
the outside of the beans.

Panning by my hand.

By means of wax added to sugar
the inside of his ear is to be the second
outside of the candy.

In order to test the validity of the flavoring,
he will only be allowed to eat the earwax
flavored ones and the unflavored ones
pulled from his ear.

The cook said, touche.

Lost Boys

The scenarios in an unnamed country,
in mountains, in mud brick,
in concrete city with check points
and monuments
and the number of civilian deaths always
vastly outnumbered the rest.

Success was ruthlessness seemed no limit.

The scenarios when, what had happened
was unbearable, the battle was
to forget the weight of weeks, all consuming
and low as a stone lodged in throat
must be so secure.

He was all plan of persuasion,
that the police had vanished, the barrier
is unmanned, so comes the astonishing thing:
this city rules the world,
the standards, and the low dead hiss, then a break.

Bed of Ecology IX

Because the chicken
Broth and lack of boy toy cook
The beautiful soup

The stock was poured into a saucepan and placed over medium-high heat. Then the smaller flavorings were added. The heat was turned down to medium-low and the stock and flavorings were allowed to simmer for fifteen minutes. Then the smaller flavorings were removed by means of a slotted spoon and some of the scallions were added to the stock. It was all allowed to simmer for five minutes. Some of the scallions were reserved to add green tourmaline rings to garnish.

One-quarter cup of stock was scooped from the soup. The cornstarch was whisked into it in a small bowl. This mixture was whisked back into the soup and was simmered for a minute or two to take away the starchy taste. The eggs were whisked together with the cornstarch in a small bowl, while the soup was brought down to a bare simmer. The eggs were drizzled into the broth. Drizzle was defined somewhere, not here thought.

A fork was held over the bowl and the eggs were poured (and they strained) through the tines. With the other hand, the soup was whisked gently. And happening continuously was the holding and pouring and whisking until the little bowl was emptied. The soup was allowed to stand for a few seconds to cook the eggs. The soup was topped with scallions and served as soon as possible to remind the diner of cat's eye tourmaline and jade.

Lost Boys

To have vanished evidence, no evidence,
nothing at all under
his breath of gin and tonic sunshine.

Read his world between the green
trees and the great slums and shanties of the city,
millions of others out there.

His fascination with burning said
he wanted a sadhu.

He has a book with holy men with saffron
robes and ash-covered bodies.

Lost Beans II

And panning again
by his ear drums is the scientist
not omnipotent to the subject
of the experiment? He will
not be allowed to clean his ears
out for a whole week. The disgusting
exists on a continuum with the cute
jelly beans are his favorites. He will
be tied to the bed and blindfolded
and unflavored jelly beans will
be shoved into his right ear
and then the left. Would not
medium sized marshmallows be
the means to make him smile more?

Well, a hundred years ago, a jelly bean
was better known as a dandy than a candy,
jack and the beanstalk indeed,
the thought already made him smile.

Lost Boys

And beards even to be buried
head first in the ground, more sounds,
he said, the lowest-caste skin and
the bright saris worn
by pauses drawing breath.

Some tea on the side of the road,
poverty makes it hard to look,
look to know what was looking at straws,
what patterns this nature
somewhere a figure suicides.

The boys are younger
and the numbers are greater, pause
does for a moment or two,
the psychology of the abandoned child
is of concern as weapon.

The report cites vast numbers
dispossessed in the third world of instability:
Lagos, Port-au-Prince, Kinshasa, Kabul
on the one hand the other
that defy wonder.

All the cities, the boy children
he would see waiting and watching eyes,
so many boys watching him,
the modern age of Baghdad, the crowd
of boys standing amid smoke.

And fire their eyes filled with a serious
watching and remembering
(past impervious)
and then hands that came out of darkness,
hands to take, to look.

He has the same dark hair,
and he has changed much and more

withdrawn
the bright, and black with figures not natural
shows four figures in black.

One of the black figures has entered
and is talking to the children,
all the black figures are back, and one
of the children. Looking on,
pause, the background
has intense red flames or sunset?

Pause, the chimney leans
as windows are missing bricks,
two bodies and blood is vividly shown on bodies,
the tree itself resembles a tangle of black.

Wire the sky is full of circling
birds, is demented pause traumatized
(he was very evasive as volatile about the boy)
and his withdrawal from the world.

The boy is overflowing something waiting
to spill out somewhere
he said, the other boy and
that this boy was friends with pretending
drawing the boy he was talking about.

Even the pen and paper tried
and tried asking why he had gone,
in a low voice he said, find, and only find him,
was what he said he looked in the eye,
he said.

CO2 Lost Boys Black Squiggles

The black chairs folding
as bats as black squiggles to
fight against letting
the soft left and the right lace
be covered in dust
as happiness sleeps upside
down. The shadow of
all bats was there standing guard
until the stunned thing
returned to itself and flew
away the wings of bats
are articulated. Like
human hands the wing
membrane will regrow from the
small tears from the claws
of Sunday (as the
cats on the farm were named for
the day of the week).

I am the mother of all
bats: mouse tailed bats and
smoky bats and ghost faced bats.

Lost Boys

Aggressive as the drawings of dark figures
of threat of terrorism of everything (of shadow).

He filled sheet after sheet of paper with
(drawings often and often drew a figure in green
in the tops of a tree playing.)

He plays his pipe (and the boys run and answer)
filling the sky with bird shapes to fight.

Fight more and more squiggles, the sky there is
the war is here, (no war here) there is the boy
had said, his pen working faster and faster.

He drew insect-like soldiers in helmets moving,
sometimes, the soldiers wearing fairy wings or
playing the flute, casting him into a sluggish
twilight world driven to building sand castles.

Exploring rock pools, signs open sky, and cries of the circling
seagulls left the weather still, the
sea flat.

If the wind had been sucked from the world, to
shake the feeling as fast as frightening,
overtaking everyone on the motorway as fast as
he had to.

The burning filled his eyes, the pair left (to
hold) to him everything had been biding time,
lost, in all the things turned in his hand
withdrawn.

He would make drawings of soldiers he used,
beads of sweat on his forehead, the bad
atmosphere, the same bed is water and garden,
wide open is not right before bed.

Lost Beens

after Sonja Vitow

A postcard of a koala
and then a video where he was
unzipping himself in the dark,
the third vagina is not given.
The hollows grown into a pattern
of raspberries see multiple
fruiting bodies to the east of here
read blackberries in black bird
duck things. Think of the buttons
and the beans. If my heart
were a stone, what stone would
it be, but a dinosaur bone?

Gone green and tan with age,
beens gone tender with age.

If my heart were a stone,
what stone would it be, but
a dragon egg? The father of all
dragon eggs, gold then red because
bird chromosomes make males
the homogametic sex. A postcard
of a komodo dragon and then
a video where the monitor was
unzipping the deoxyribonucleic acid
in the dark, the sex of the offspring
was not given. Hollow is the
patterning of ova and raspberries.

Lost Boys

Top and bottom go outside
to see that the gate
to the communal gardens was wide
open need was bright with
a full moon and cold in the middle,
see he was so, and his eyes were closed,
and his mouth was open.

He was breathing funny because
his body got so heavy, see,
and so forget like a dream,
in the pause that follows trying
to work something out before speaking
the pause, sense pause, tired pause,
well more boys all pause.

Fascinating pause,
look into the garden again,
he feels his head spinning, he can
remember under the trees
falling the memory of a dream: masks,
scarves, bodies in dark sheets, he shakes
his head, the boys he remembers
feet scampering down a hotel corridor
he must keep, (must press on) he was.

Bed of Ecology X

oysters as blood as
oysters as blood oranges
as sapphires as rough
brown pebbles as oranges
as bled dry the heart
as the raven as rough brown
breadcrumbs as sapphires
as hard to say as giant
as red sap against
rough brown pebbles as dragon
tree bark as sapphires
as dragon testicles as
as fire opals as
forever blood oranges

        on the barrage rocks
       the mother of all ravens
      dropped a rough brown bead

Lost Boys

The majority are boys on the cusp of puberty,
others are older, missing balls and bulldozers,
but as many were living waiting to go
somewhere clearly relished.

It was hard to tell a small explosion,
entering the second floor,
an entire floor soaked in petrol,
flames up the building followed by no fatality,
no matter how savage the dozens
and dozens having to wait behind.

Masses of too much violent computer games,
and internet porn, to keep an open mind
opposite, floodlights shone over
three dozen boys sitting cross-legged,
lost and defiant and angry, pause fierce eyes.

Disgust was pause, tearing limb
from limb with bare hands and the air
simmered with the pictures, the more like animals,
more distortion as being tuned in
and out in rooms crammed with mattresses,
christmas lights, and walls covered with writing.

World from computer games, he pauses,
hard to, hard to, there was so much
there: sunglasses, home-made swords, and nail bombs
as the boys were searched,
and their hands were tied with cord,
almost all the boys were white,
and the police were writing it all down (wait at play).

Aggressive

A grey horse has white
hair. The grey pilgrim,
greyhame, he will have
killed hundreds of the
dragons in his days. In
medias res, read the star
of green sapphire prob-
lematic. The metallic gre-
en wings of flies litter at
rest; leaves the grey to
return as white mold
and maggots they will
begin again. The music
in medias res is a grey
sieve for straining the
midnight green. He is
aggressive. As much as
moths and mosquitoes
strain against the screen
there is the bright white
space in the middle of
the midwinter night.

Lost Boys

To be clear, see here, the police have it as well,
potential. See the dead horse buying it. His mind,
his flight had no ransom note all, for nothing
minds a little more please. Do pause that rustling
noise on, and on it is better to keep his eyes on the
surface and nothing. Nothing at all he hears:
pause have pause, since pause his pause, this
pause, pause, his pause, pause, pause he was so
pause, always pause. Always and burning, eve-
ning in the garden as the sun went down, burnt
until there was nothing. The pictures just ash in
the grass that never was sometimes he still had
dreams with the garden with the other moon whi-
te on their skin. But, whenever he want to look
the lawn was ringing, it was hard work it carried.
Pause the rain, the heat dried out, then to be
thinking as well minimal, the climate worrying
over the boys.

Fuck Connecticut

Steel yourself against the dandelions,
the leaves, not the heads, look like the teeth of lions.
Black, red, brown manes of stone ground mustard to dress
put the gray inside and make up. A fork instead,

the leaves, not the heads, looks like the truth of lions
must hear yellow insides. Stainless outside
puts the sieve aside, and takes up a whisk instead.
Stainless is never the hand, honey, sea salt, and thyme

must. Here gray insides. Mustard outside
red wine vinegar, and black pepper into the salad
stand the less. Never never land hun, eye see salt and time to
steel yourself against the dandy lions.

Lost Boys

The nation was two minds in the end (pause)
inaudible to new pipelines and refineries.

Oil, needs oil, it keeps flowing as
(much) oil as possible, oil for pause helicopters,
it was all something too late to know
what it was like exciting as it was so hot.

See right across the city was quiet,
then was gunfire red and green,
from darkened swathes of the night slicing the sky,
five in orange flashes,
the horizon dull and rattling the windows pause.

Power it was, pause the heart the dread and
the horror until dawn, days the view he remembered
the bad taste of many millions of barrels of oil
would be flowing on the fourth day
outside the green jeeps the colors all grey.

Dust and intense hot sunshine had been precise,
concrete see the places looted,
these ruined this relentless everything was
happening, and fuel or water was dangerous
two hundred meters away.

A balloon of dust and fire rose fast and
the blast pushed pause dust and glass
and sight of the fire was bleeding was bleeding.

The blast had great black smoke rising and the ground
was scattered with broken glass pause.

Campanula Rapunculus

Rap pun Rapunsel
let down your hair that I climb
thy bittersweet stair

Little bell, little turnip let winter-sweet be everywhere. Companion with bread, with red violent to light blue bellflower. To the bitterness of turnips not yet boiled. They come in purple and fairytales, but that doesn't make them perfect, only nec-essary, not sufficient. The prince possesses a horse; that is his charm. Jump the moon, oh mine. The mare is a champion that wore blue and red ribbons on her head and a braid in her tail.

What is a horse a metaphor for? For using the dead to swipe the flies from the living, for walking home to meanwhile farm. Whi-ther they go, the six lanceolate leaves are not given.

Lost Boys

And the sound increases drowning. His voice filters out the desert circulating yet unidentified parts forward is something else. In the remote islands in the slums reports from the CIA claim.

The new forest vanishing all vanished and all unusual.

The police in the end settle on a crime committed the leader thing and nothing in the end is man was behind it. Claimed he was persuaded, saying: over over world and the authorities.

Think back to the new forest case, fashion causes that sort of thing to stop motorways and airports and the rebellious ones found the underground. The woods dissolving into a wall static.

It takes a minute or two. Turning into a palimpsest the plastic between he puts in the machine. The voice he hears more than whisper in the background waves of background white intercut with (other) stranger has been in brutal fashion.

Hushed and close sounds so high.

Breaking in the container there was no light and it was hard to breath sometimes, sometimes time would pass inside: one was wanted, one had seen his name in the sky, one is many coming. Cuts in the border. The container, the air, and the light was so again the mountain was fresh and cold peaks. The sun was setting. The sky hard blue ran through the earth waiting.

Lived Data

Data observes his cat dreaming.
The android wonders what a 24th century feline
might have to dream about, before he lays down
and turns the lights down to dream himself.
The frosting is blue as a medicine or science
uniform.
Data is ordered to answer the phone, and he
does so, then fails to wake for his duty shift for
the first time.
The internal chronometer of the android has
malfunctioned.
Any anomaly in his neural nets is pretty strange,
so instead, he heads to the holodeck to discuss
the phallic symbolism of knives.
What is the technological problem?
What about the cat, what about the lion king he
dreams he is?
He prefers feline supplement number twenty-
five and water and a sandbox and you must talk
to him, tell him he is a pretty cat and a good cat.
Do not mention the litter of lizard-like things or
the sex change.
When in the holodeck of data's dreams, the
captain accepts a slice of cake and asks the
android, what kind of cake is this?
Data states that it is a cellular peptide cake with
mint frosting.
Then the android dreams of Freud, and he
interprets the inter-phasing organisms without
commenting on orgasms before data is
dismembered.
Something to do with the plasma conduit.

The timing the ringing returns to the command
to answer the ringing.
The android must respond to his enemies and the
enemies of his friends by shrieking this high-
pitched sound until the waking dream ends.
What is wrong with the lived experience of
data?

Lost Boys

(The guide to the castle long and hard.)

~~waves overlapping~~
~~over and separating~~
~~new over sounds young~~

Soldiers came late, breaking the darkness was full of soldiers goggles, hiding their eyes gleaming in the moonlight in the other room in the dust. The full heat of the sun was burning back and asked one place in place in the desert thousands. Soldiers hear screaming red and white lights the sand.

~~cuts in continues~~
~~noises and dominance high-~~
~~pitched as increases~~

~~in intensity~~
~~like tinnitus, wincing it~~
~~something like disgust~~

~~dialogues to lead~~
~~him back to feelings about~~
~~things never to hand~~

~~strained tight against the~~
~~background sounds of someone tied~~
~~and trying to move~~

Mind or something like that. Dammit. Something with a masochistic theme pause message or something stop. The boy has sat as near as he can to very, and he was standing over close his crotch was only aggression. Look. This boy was a mop of floppy hair. He was wearing faded jeans and a jumper must pause like to think. And the men were all white men standing against the cold in scarves, another card, long leather boots almost tempted. Almost eating sweets and smoking and swearing that might well tell.

hot wind blowing leaves
desolate places leak to
fill the listening

Sense is so much more flexible. So much more, so open, so much
easier to pause his body. How far to pause those damn cards,
and each morning one more joins the others standing outside,
and outside waiting. About outside, coming back to the bones
the bodies stay.

pause stop hiss start is
drowned out rhythmic must be the
train inaudible

Around and inaudible inside and buried dark the standards.
Start more than ever, this has never happened inside in the sha-
dows. Sometimes so hard to tell the way they hide with scarves
the others, all the others are waiting. Waiting to take the lost
must.

stop start stop pause hiss
start breaks nothing just a hiss
a desert static

CO2 Lost Boys Purple Skittles

Wife of brain taught me to add ginger root because the mucilaginous pulp is the sweet of the chocolate fruit.

Wife of brain crushes up raw cacao for her protein shake for extra magnesium for her muscles, well, magnesium gems.

What does it mean when an elemental poet says beautiful alkaline earth metals?

The answer is not raw peridot.

Magnesium filings bursting into flames in the damp.

Wife of fireworks, what is lost with roasting the beans the purple wish?

Purple as sunburn bitter dark, dark bitter, bitter sweet, sweet bitter is the flavor of the bean.

The color is telling of the ripening.

Sweating the seeds, sweating away the pulp, sweating yields the beans.

Thick with the origin, the seeds themselves are lavender pale to brown wishes purple dark to pod has the leather red rind.

Wife of brain loves the smell of leather, the life of the chorus is a cultural anthropologist.

Lost Boys

Cold striated, his thoughts would cool the things
around the rolling camera and screen circling an
alien planet, scanning the surface of his skin and
canyon.

Noting as he rose (the man opened the door) to
keep the man was simple for the ground.

An orb-nerve dangling between abstract and chrome.

Only a static sort of aspic of the nerves one day,
then the next, the pain was never any less.

He drank at it like a part of him had been bound
and had ebbed, but a fraction.

Bitterness and swearing and being sucked from
the building.

The window air sucked from his lungs.

Devour the sky, the cascade of white against
grey against blue.

He would remember the oily smoke as sweat was
not easy for ominous, the cloud had to dissipate
as missing eyes filled with sense of something
much less.

A new phenomenon from the litter gathered
around the ominous sign.

His first thought had been (the message) have
you been a bad boy? (this missive in blue ink)
on the wall outside.

       A slippery oil slick of the nerves he saw
(following at a distance) like a shadow skin.

Not Lost I

the ghosts of salmon
millions of fish escaping
to swim in the sea

something like easter eggs
that he juggled not
something like testicles that
he juggled like
tinker bell her fairy lights

to miss the pewter
iolite punning and not
sleeping yet waltzing

ashes floating slowly down
the train the long pipe
that feeds the salmon alive
almost saving wild

fish stocks except the sea lice
antibiotics
the trespassing seals shot dead

Lost Boys

Have you been a bad boy in bold
red, the rising head of a monster?

      raised

Have you been a bad boy
and moved into his he and turned on
his he slid into the machine and recorded.

      He could make out vibrating pixels
      to make him look like an insect.

The eyes as the visor and filter
of a gas mask being removed
and for the first time the camera moved.

Zooming to the face of the face reminded him.

He was coming moving arms moving
and moved he came
holding the camera moving the screen.

      finished

      nauseous

He wanted again
and again in the sweat and the tight.

He kept stopping and pausing he was seeing
like the man, the night, the night was young.

Not Lost II

as first world a poem
as blue velvet cake because
dolphin awareness
swims through your veins like a fish
in the sea, follow
the red food coloring not
coloring the red
velvet the first day of spring

the magenta cake
my sister wanted beet root
because of cancer
vanilla and beaver tails
yellow the wish and
the swish of their castor sacs
aphrodisiac

Lost Boys

Drip drip with no end,
and no night under inside
methods had the dark
on more diamond eyed. He
headed to midnight,
have you been a bad boy, a
flat stomach, and a
gas mask covered face?
From the camera
the stirring within him, he
was paralyzed hands.
Have you been a bad boy would
lead to a dead end
dissolved to the phone he found.

Not Lost III

I saw the ghosts of
oysters drift away as smoke
as slivers as I
saw the body of the white
rabbit. My present
is shellfish, sand, and ashes.

Not seeding oyster-
like tumors on computed
tomography, and
the position emission
tomography   ghost,
not testing for the grey-white
pearls in the tissue.

I saw the silk inclusions
thickening the air
before the velvet to blue
to violet wish
blue with medium dark tones
Serendip is home.

Lost Boys

No more gloom to the armored
jeeps, guarded with sunburnt heads
that seemed too small, in visor-like
glass hid their eyes, day, and
nerves even he remembered past
the blasted vehicle bristling with
antennae and machine guns.

A camera following as a second
camera watched as he walked the
deep red carpet swallowing his
black and white photos a whole cut
into open windows, dark inside his eyes.

His penis of his pale body a box
had been a cigarette he tried again,
he was living, doing many things,
the room no longer as warm as it
had plumes of smoke dissolved
around he knew, know, know, no,
know, know, or not at all cold.

Not Lost IV

My present is three,
the princes of Serendip:
mother, father, and
the one who gifted you the
jacket. Let the scarf
be a turban when in doubt.

Let the last voyage
of somebody the sailor,
author of the sot
weed factor not rolling
either. When in doubt
throw Grobstein on the table

of Sinbad and wait
for some permission to smoke.

Lost Boys

Since the sound of rain in the morning, it was
watching the rain, was the rain was the same as
always, sleek black water asking have you been
a bad boy?

He was against the glass endless grey, one
glance at his journey, the silvery drawing the
sky on black brick walls, rising over the
lights, the blackness of the clouds and the eyes.

His eyes sometimes the light of the tower was
the air, was melting into the green square, to do
it was not as if he was riding down.

A pound into the machine in his hand had
sounded his head was turning hot and humid
and he could hide, everything had everything
had the dust had determined hands.

He remembered the heat of the ropes, and too
and too and too and he had as he writhed in the
heat, his body humiliated empty moments bright
of dreams.

Ghosts whispering in the room.

He heard the nothing coming and everything
was very clear, and was nearly over and down to
head, and down was everywhere and all the
light hitting him, and there was nothing tight
against the bright.

Everything was so quiet.

On the ground, lie down on the ground, on the
gun pressed against his head was the dirt and the
water, the dirty blue of being that morning not
nothing.

Not Lost V

Overwhelming how
it makes me want to cry all
over an ostrich

Lost Boys

back the red oil
the black it tracking the risks
he read the method

Angry for a part is here a part of here after the mountains in the
main square all the forgotten things are here the rainbow and the
tape reels. The old buildings overgrown with yellow moss and
skinny cats for understanding the world and the dirty canal
paths and the deepest thing, the sun beats down red with shad-
ows high into here eyed. After Istanbul, Samarkand, New York,
Naples, Shenzhen, and Tangiers find here. Upside down ready
skin is darker and each day it gets darker wear the grease and
dust is under painted blue in the blood poison of frogs. The boy
who was once the boy who was once the boy who was once old
cast aside like the old clothes the shadow of the lost. The wild,
the never-never, the lost boys of the old man who lives in the
mountains. Tower there in the far eyes and voices and forbidden
men. Soldiers will stand. Oil will an army of police hunting dogs
and helicopters running into the sewers. Waited in the mud: the
grass, the leaves, the sapling, the moss, the birds, the rabbits, the
deer inside swimming in blood. Everywhere that bitter petrol
station air. All the false gods eyes like metal can make shapes in
the heart it is only this is only.

alien too too
too long silvery lost boys
in the bonfire sky

eyes of sticks and stones
wiped away walls silvery
sound of the castle

The rain, the rumble, and the flash of the hot winds. The clouds
that come with dust and the drone of cicadas pink strike the
morning. Pine and litter the gutters. Falling leaves dust the

seaside town adding on a whitewashed wall. In the night singing, the small rhythms from the tower beyond the high towers and the land beyond the fortress flower petals unfolding saffron, mint, and jasmine. The beautiful eyes of the silver coast forest.

Not Lost VI

I saw the ghost of the white
flemish giant was
two boxes of halloumi
later. I knew to
use a lighter as bottle-
opener in the
time before the zeroing
event. This time   then
the white rabbit would eat with
ease, nineteen peppers,
and you besides. The lettuce
heads under the sky.

I saw   not   clouding over
another flat white.

Lost Boys

black and black and black
and shadow the black-white sky

out the window with
bright with the intensity

of beautiful was
thinner and whiter about

eyes grey to see the
in eyes without limit for

a moment his eyes
like moths before a light on

his phone windows are
night like nearly so many

soup baked sea bass and
new potatoes the main screen

charmed his eyes and no
cameras and he drank and

listened and noticed
too much time would be online

the second and the
funny thing was always that

screen that damn machine
glass at the back of his head

moment no one said
anything without tasting

first the computer
had hundreds of files saved and
the funny thing was.

Not Lost VII

after 11/4/17

Holding the pattern
on the back of the oyster
shell, is the pattern
on the outside of the bear
skin.   My borrowed skin.

This forest is a grey sieve,
of mint little wish
filters, not slicing through time.

Diamond, not key
to stone animals bearing
spoons,   as shellfish skin.

Never, never, vast station
in the bay waters,
dear bear, rest if a grey sieve.

Lost Boys

the orange light and
lonesome night a light rain was

falling with drowning
lights out this night was silent

white in the mirror
as he was the mother arms

moment of body
spring of his hair and kissing

his resistance his
slipping into his trousers

and he though that part
(everything) his desire

had his his his his
his his his his his his his

his heart was Tuesday
window white robes quite dirty

and hair was darker
dirty as he was older

and he had a knife
a silver blade was handsome

of dust such white teeth
know a glass of milk his hand

and honey his skin
luminous in the soaking

shivering in his
eyes the grass soaking his feet

shivering as rain
fell through the trees and drumming
against the window

Not Lost VIII

The answer is red-
      orange as salmon roe cast
            shadows on the ghost of her. Here is
the biologist
      developmental never
            never embryos. Deuterostomes,
their central nervous
      system lies on the dorsal
            side, protostomes on the ventral side.
As promised upside-
      down, the kitten is twisting
            the hearts of deuterostomes always
lie on the ventral
      side. See how similar the
            body plan can invert the mouth and
anus position.
      The abject biology
            promises that forever we will
never get better
      at growing up and learning
            to lie. From the heart to the head, not
losing the red year
      the lantern, the history,
            someone else's salmon dip as well.
Sour the cream of ghosts
      anassa kata, kalo
            kale, ia ia ia nike, bryn mawr
bryn mawr bryn mawr...

Lost Boys

eyes the mirror he
had the wild eyes of night like
oil and steel clean

In the ruins by the enemy tank, the ambush watched the flames.
The air an hour or so later, the drone circling around sugar and
    smoking for days.
The enemy played amid the ruins (many) had his eyes.
Among the fries, sometimes, would play the voices of mothers
    over the speakers calling for their boys to come, come
    home, come.
No mother was really the drone.
Southwards, and an hour later, warned of dust trails in the
    distance gathered.
Kalashnikovs, M-16s, ammunition, pistols, grenades, scimitars,
    crossbows, and the Russian shoulder-mounted rocket
    launcher they had.
Bottles filled with petrol and sulfuric acid were loaded.
Most robes of white or black (both shades) soiled by weeks of
    fighting faces of the same color.
Pirate and superhero had been odd continued.
His red cape more battered than before narrow shoulders.
The enemy, they had no symbol, but blue or white or red hand
    open and the fingers spread as wide as the troops.
The blasted walls and burnt out petrol stations clapping from
    and final minutes.
Growing armored prayers to a pipe.
Hoping it was true, that the white fumes would give powers to
    fight what is happening, is how it is.

reaching into his
he have you been a bad boy
making his number

Not Lost IX

Not my sushi roll,
dear oyster toadfish swimming
foghorn-like fish. I
miss the hum of opsanus
tau, the ugly toad
lies still, and waiting for prey,
grey-black camouflaged
fins and all silent. Oyster
cracker here yellow
oh wishes brown the butter,
bar dog, bare the young
toadfish stay attached to their
yolk. They do not learn
to swim until their yolk is
translated into
energy, not lost. Learning
to swim in space? Please
trade a handstand for kissing
underwater is
choking on the father of
all oyster toadfish,
there eyes are a purple-black.

Lost Boys

His whispered fingers were inside
his mouth, white teeth and warm mouth
of his coca-cola breath, all the flashing teeth
saw the camera in the corner turned.

His humiliation filled his gas mask breathing
filled the room, he whimpered
watching as faint as white.

His breathing seemed from the opposite
wall, he tried to turn away,
he could see the room was squirming, the
newspaper strips shifting into alphabet.

He was sweating hard, the wet with him,
the material clinging
to his skin mean. He saw that look he had
that way of looking as if meeting
this morning an emergency
with eyebrows meeting in the middle.

What the hood and the darkness second,
on the wall he was,
his hands grasping sheets stained.

A long wand in gloved hands his head,
and his mouth filled with blood,
bleeding see he had been watching the
screen and the orange falling, the city never
to be seen again.

Not Lost X

When in doubt throw the
shadow of the black rabbit
on the table with
irony on irony.

When all is said and
sugar plums are not burning
but turning turning.

Bear to berries purple-black
place to Lanka to
Sihala to Lakdiva
to Serendib to
Ceylon sapphire. When in doubt
throw the ghost of the
white rabbit on the table.

Lost Boys

(most of) time wore the gas
mask, insisted on it and the low
rasp of breathing.

Sometimes there in the room,
sometimes in the cages, some-
times with ass, sometimes gas
mask and mucus and sperm,
sometimes people watched.

Sometimes watched cameras
were recording on a screen
hands around neck, sometimes
there were men in the cages like
groveling animals. Sometimes
wore the gas mask, sometimes
fucked in front of the men.

Times tried to escape was the
shame was too much lost until
the air turned black and heavy
and sparks eyes.

Sometimes would find naked
and shivering shit all over
body shaking and bleeding the
walls more animal captured on
the screens see faces face eyes
filled it was no use and the bod-
ies found in the morning in the
parks and more.

Sometimes (in the quiet mo-
ments) had been military, see all
the soldiers shining in the sun
sometimes not.

Later wore the gas mask, the room was empty of paper in the machine in the morning.

Time filled with dust, the sky was hazy, the heat was overwhelming the bleached sky and his eyes were missing the black flies in the distance, then silence a line of walls, and a hand print on a wall of dust, cordite, and oil.

All the lost boys, the wild boys, the dinosaur boys, boys (in the dusty streets) burning burning the oil under a white sky.

Pity the Room its Forced Embrace of the Animals

after Matthea Harvey

Analogous:
Aquatic reptiles go,
Alligators
Are less
Aggressive than crocodiles.

Banana to you the stars are
Balls of gas
Burning millions of miles away, it is always gas,
Bubbling,

Cocoa I wanted. And I wanted a
Cat and you gave me a
Crocodile.

Dress in
Drag and
Do the hula with
Dragon fruit red lips
Discuss the
Death of cells,
Differentiation, and kittens in

Evolutionary developmental biology,
Egg drop soup which came first the crocodile or the
Egg?

Fireflies that got stuck in that big blue wish black thing
Future perfect, present imperfect.

Grovel not
Gravel before the
Great kings of the past.

Hakuna matata.

Ice bats,
Impressed upon by neighboring crystals
In the

Jungle, the mighty
Jungle the lion sleeps tonight. It is safer to feed any cat
Jellybeans than onions. I wanted a

Kitten and you gave me a crocodile, the crocodiles did not
Kill.

Let gas masks be gray,
Let us say they are the outside of oyster shells,
Let the king sleep here.

Mouth the apple Pumbaa and be not afraid
My teeth and ambitions are bared, be prepared for the
Mouth of the crocodile.

Never (never) return
No onions

Onions will kill lions
Only if the universe repeats itself,
Only if
Oysters repeat
Only if

Pi repeats as
Peter
Piper
Pan
Pied
Palatal flap at the back of the mouth blocks water from the
                              crocodile stomach.

Queen Nala, the lion cub with the complexion of
quince fruit.

Remember and
Roar and
Red and black and the aphrodisiac.

Slimy yet
Satisfying, this is
Sleeping with the lion king. This is

So
Sad but great the micro-state where the hero and monster come.

Telling stories of drinking
Turkish apple
Tea.

Undifferentiated bits of the
Universe.

Violent rock candy to feed
Violet passions to feed.

Wildebeest stampede does not trample him,
When the
World turns its back on you, turn your back on the
World.

Xenon inert gas, noble gas opposite the
Xenoblast bounded by the faces found in neighboring crystals.

Yes I see the crystals inside the metamorphic rock are rock candy to you;
Yellow is golden delicious apples is bananas is quinces.

Zazu who is trapped between rock and ribcage,
Zoo animals are prostitutes paid in food.

Published in the United Kingdom in November 2017 by

HVTN Press,
www.hvtn.co.uk

ISBN: 978-1-9998670-0-3

Cover Design by *Open Air Design*

Thanks are due to the following magazines, in which many of these poems first appeared:

> *Backlash, Haverthorn Magazine, Junction Box, Serendip Studio, The Seethographer, Visual Verse*

TEXAS

Baseball

A LONE STAR DIAMOND HISTORY FROM
TOWN TEAMS TO THE BIG LEAGUES

CLAY COPPEDGE

THE
History
PRESS

Published by The History Press
Charleston, SC 29403
www.historypress.net

Copyright © 2012 by Clay Coppedge
All rights reserved

First published 2012

Manufactured in the United States

ISBN 978.1.60949.598.5

Library of Congress Cataloging-in-Publication Data

Coppedge, Clay.
Texas baseball : a Lone Star diamond history from town teams to the big leagues /
Clay Coppedge.
p. cm.
Includes bibliographical references and index.
ISBN 978-1-60949-598-5
1. Baseball--Texas--History. 2. Baseball teams--Texas--History. 3. Baseball
players--Texas--Biography. I. Title.
GV863.T4C67 2012
796.35709764--dc23
2012008740

For Tori, who allowed me to share my love of the game with her

CONTENTS

CONTENTS

OPENING DAYS

In 1861, some enterprising Houston gentlemen formed the Houston Base Ball Club to promote the relatively new sport locally, much as clubs in New York had done, but the Civil War postponed organized baseball, along with everything else in the country. The conflict did, in that peculiar cross-cultural way of wars, help spread the game to the South and to Texas. Confederates probably learned it either as prisoners of war or while guarding Union prisoners. Abraham Lincoln was a baseball player. In fact, he was playing a game of sandlot ball when he formally received word that he had won the presidential nomination in 1860. He told the messenger, "Tell the gentlemen they will have to wait a few minutes till I get my turn at bat."

Two years after the end of the Civil War, on April 21, 1867, the Houston Stonewalls slaughtered the Galveston Robert E. Lees by a score of 35–2 in a friendly game of "base ball," as it was usually spelled in those days. The game took place on the thirty-first anniversary of the Battle of San Jacinto, the site of the battle where Sam Houston's ragtag army of volunteers defeated Mexican general Santa Anna's troops and thus earned Texas's independence from Mexico. Just as there was no mercy rule on the battlefield, apparently none was in place at this baseball game either.

Stories that Abner Doubleday was at the game and even played in it are not true, nor is the myth that Doubleday invented the game of baseball. Doubleday spent some time in Texas after the war—first in Galveston and later in west Texas—but he was in Galveston as a member of an occupying army. Even if he had been at the game, and even if he had invented it, it is

Above: Kids took to baseball early, as shown by this 1895 team near La Grange. *Fayette Heritage Museum and Archives.*

Left: Abner Doubleday did a lot of things, but inventing the game of baseball was not one of them. *Library of Congress.*

doubtful that the Stonewalls or Lees would have invited a Union officer to play for them. It has been said of Doubleday that the only thing he ever started was the Civil War—he fired the first cannon shot in defense of Fort Sumter.

Doubleday left behind a lot of correspondence of significant historical value, but nowhere does he mention, even in passing, the game he is said to have invented. At the time he was said to have invented it—1839—he was at West Point. Army records indicate that Doubleday was "correct in deportment, social and communicative with his companions…but adverse to outdoor sports."

Doubleday wasn't anointed inventor of baseball until fourteen years after he died, when sporting goods magnate Albert Goodwill Spalding appointed a commission to find the origin of the game that was helping to make him rich. He appointed Abraham G. Mills to chair the Mills Commission, which concluded, "The first scheme for playing baseball, according to the best evidence obtainable to date, was devised by Abner Doubleday at Cooperstown, New York, in 1839."

The commission's main source for the story was a letter from one Abner Graves of Cooperstown, who, at age ninety, was convicted of killing his wife and was sentenced to spend the rest of his life in an asylum for the criminally insane.

Most likely, the commission determined that it was impossible to establish who actually invented baseball. It might have concluded, correctly, that the game was based somewhat on the English games of rounders and cricket and that those games were based on other games that might have gone back as far as the fourteenth century. With a deadline looming, it might have simply decided to trace the origins back to a West Point graduate and war hero who, without something a little extra special added to his name, might not be remembered by history at all.

Most of the baseball played in Texas in the late nineteenth century consisted of "town" teams. Baseball was a welcome diversion and an inexpensive form of recreation at a time and place when there was little of either. Nearly every town had at least one baseball team, and some had as many as three, which were usually divided along racial lines: white, black and Hispanic. A team from one town would play a team from another town for bragging rights, and people from local communities would gather on Sunday afternoons to watch the local lads play a little ball. This was the heart of the game in Texas and in the wider world for the first decades of the game's existence. In *Baseball: The People's Game*, baseball historian Harold Seymour wrote about how the game brought communities and neighborhoods together:

LaGrange baseball team, circa 1915. *Fayette Heritage Museum and Archives.*

The town baseball team acted as a cohesive agent in the community. Symbolizing the town's quality and providing a clear-cut means of demonstrating it, the team ignited local pride...Most teams, at least at the outset, were composed wholly or in part of home town players, the fans' own neighbors and even relatives, and so made for a close bond between team and residents.

In Texas, a lot of the first baseball games were played in pastures where sheep or cattle kept the grass at a playable level. Women fried chicken and prepared jars of lemonade for the game, and people came from miles around to see the local nine take on another town team. Bragging rights were always on the line. When something other than bragging rights was at stake, it wasn't unusual for towns to hire a ringer, somebody from a nearby semipro team, to take over one of the positions, usually pitcher.

Not too long after baseball became a popular pastime, the game went from being strictly a form of fun and recreation to a legitimate business enterprise with owners, bosses, employees and customers, otherwise known as fans; the notion of paying players and charging admission to the game took root in many an entrepreneurial mind.

The National Association, formed in 1871, took hold in New York and Philadelphia and morphed into the National League in 1876. That same year, the International Association was formed in hopes that people in small towns might pay to watch professional baseball, too. Other like-minded leagues soon followed, and in one, the Midwest League, a fair-to-middling utility player named John McCloskey emerged.

McCloskey played all nine positions on the field at one time or another and would also umpire and manage. He formed his own barnstorming team, the Joplin Independents, and brought it to Texas for a series of exhibition games against teams from Fort Worth, Waco and Austin. They knocked off the Fort Worth and Waco teams with little trouble, but McCloskey got a tip from a bellman in Austin that something was up: the local organizers had brought in some ringers from the Southern Association to play the Independents.

The Independents held on to beat the Austin ringers, but McCloskey was impressed by the passion that would lead somebody to load up a team of ringers for an exhibition game. He got the idea that such passion might support a professional baseball league.

From that notion came the Texas League, first called the Texas League of Base Ball Clubs, which played its first game on April 1, 1888, in Houston. The term "Texas Leaguer," meant to describe a bloop single, was coined that first year and has been part of the sports lexicon ever since. The league had financial trouble from the first. Fans were rowdy and would sometimes whip out pistols and take shots at fly balls either for fun or in vain attempts to change their trajectories.

Much of the financial trouble could be traced back to the fact that neither McCloskey nor his investors knew anything about running a professional baseball league. McCloskey eschewed a leadership position in the league he helped form, choosing instead to manage the Austin Independents and play center field. The league barely made it through its first year and limped through a couple more years before it started a process of going out of business one year and starting again a year or two later. Finally, in 1902, the league opened again and this time got it right. With the exception of 1943–45, when the majority of America's young men were engaged in the war effort, the Texas League has operated ever since McCloskey got the bright idea to start it.

McCloskey umpired and managed in the Texas League and the Southern League before heading west and helping start the Pacific Coast League, where he became a manager. He got his shot at the Major Leagues in 1906, when he managed the St. Louis Cardinals, but his teams were a woeful 197-

434 from 1906 through 1908, for a paltry .312 winning percentage, the worst ever for a manager with at least 300 games. He returned to Texas and started the Rio Grande Valley League in 1914 and, true to form, managed the El Paso team in 1915. In his seventies, he helped organize the Kitty League in the Midwest. He died in 1940 from a stroke and is buried in his hometown of Louisville, Kentucky. The obituary from the *Louisville Courier* said of him:

> *Honest John never made any money from any league he organized. To effect the organization of a league, he would take the weakest town in the proposed circuit, a town nobody else wanted. Frequently, the town he took was the one to fold. He often paid players on defunct clubs out of his own pocket. And during the winter he spent his own money turning the ground into virgin baseball territory, for the planting of the seed of professional baseball.*

FOREVER YOUNGS

The first professional baseball team in America was the Cincinnati Red Legs, which formed in 1869. The Chicago White Stockings followed suit, and the National Association was formed two years later. Before long, America had a national pastime on its hands. As part of a summer game, these first professional players often worked to make a living in the off-season. Managers and owners decided the players need a period of spring training before they started playing the games for keeps. By the early part of the twentieth century, most American and National League teams were making annual treks to Texas in February and March to round the players into shape for the upcoming year.

The St. Louis Cardinals held their 1903 spring training in Dallas, and this kicked off a steady stream of teams that trained in Texas. Over the next twenty-two years, fourteen of the sixteen big-league teams would train in Texas at one time or another. San Antonio was the most popular site, but many smaller towns, including Brownsville, Cisco, Corsicana, Eagle Pass, Mineral Wells, Orange, Palestine, San Augustine, Seguin and Waxahachie, were big-league cities for a few weeks every spring.

In 1908, New York Giants manager John McGraw called the Arlington Hotel in Marlin to inquire about renting it for a few weeks starting in February. McGraw had decided that Marlin, well off the beaten path in the relatively mild climate of central Texas, would be a perfect site for his team's spring training. Not only was Marlin—or Marlin Springs, as it was sometimes called—served by three railroads, but it was also known

Members of the New York Giants walking the railroad tracks in Marlin. Life *magazine, 1963.*

far and wide as a health resort because of its hot, mineral-laden water. The town was thick with bathhouses and spas, and the hot mineral water became the city's calling card for tourism and prosperity.

Aside from the alleged health benefits of the city, Marlin didn't allow any drinking or gambling. "My idea of no setting for a pleasure party is Marlin Springs, Texas," opined New York Giants pitcher Christy Mathewson, who preferred checkers to poker anyway. Mathewson, who had a photographic memory and

New York Giants spring training photo in Marlin. *Dr. James Bryan and the Falls County Historical Commission.*

was one of the first college-educated professional ballplayers, was a checker champion. To while away the time in Marlin, he challenged all comers to checkers in the lobby of the Arlington; his winning percentage on the checkerboard was even higher than his won-lost percentage on the mound.

McGraw was a belligerent and hard-bitten individual who was among that first generation to grow up loving this newfangled game of baseball. The generation of Texans who first took up the game in earnest and fell in love with it at an early age was born just as the last vestiges of the Old West were fading into romance and mythology. Their fathers had fought in the Civil War, usually for the South. They grew up in the country and, each in his own way, discovered a game they would love for the rest of their lives. Some of those local kids were pretty good ballplayers. They were the first to step onto a field and be recognized by their peers and spectators as something special—natural athletes who could swing a bat and throw and catch a ball better and run faster than anybody else on the field. They were some of the first Texans to dream of playing baseball for a living and then to actually do so. Some of them, like Tris Speaker and Rogers Hornsby, played it as well as anybody has ever played it.

The older generation didn't always understand. John McGraw's father didn't. The boy's love of baseball was a constant source of friction between the two men. While part of baseball's mythos today centers on fathers and sons or fathers and daughters playing catch, solidifying family bonds and passing a love of the game from one generation to the next, the early ballplayers had few such warm and fuzzy experiences with their fathers. The older generation generally thought this new game of baseball was a waste of time at best and the devil's diversion at worst. McGraw's father was one of those men. A devastating family tragedy widened the gap between young John McGraw and his father.

When McGraw was twelve, his mother and four of his siblings died of diphtheria within a few weeks of one another. An already tenuous relationship with his father deteriorated further to the point of beatings. John McGraw left home when he was fourteen to live with a neighbor. Three years later, he was a professional baseball player. In 1902, he began a thirty-year stint as manager of the Giants.

McGraw was never known as an overly sentimental man or manager, but he took an interest in a stocky, aggressive outfielder from San Antonio named Ross Youngs. Born in Shiner, Ross Youngs' father up and left one day when Ross was ten. At some point not long after that, he was in San Antonio, where he was a standout in track, football and baseball; he was

New York Giants coach John McGraw. *Library of Congress.*

a member of the 1913 San Antonio High School team that won that year's state baseball championship. Youngs picked up some extra money playing baseball in the lower echelons of the minors, the bush leagues, when he was still in high school. He ended up at one point with Sherman of the Western Association, which sold his contract to the Giants. Youngs reported to spring training in Marlin in 1917, but McGraw decided the kid was too inexperienced to make the jump from the bush leagues to the Majors and sent him to Rochester in the International League for some seasoning. The first recorded mention of his nickname of "Pep" was in a Rochester newspaper, where a fan wrote a poem: "Ode to Pep Youngs."

The next spring, Pep Youngs made the trip north from Marlin to open the season with the Giants. He hit .300 or better nine of the ten years he played and compiled a lifetime batting average of .322. During the Giants' four-year run of dominance from 1921 through 1924, Youngs hit .327, .331, .336 and .356, respectively. McGraw called him "the best outfielder I ever saw." Frankie Frisch said of him, "He was the hardest-running, devil-may-care guy I ever saw. The best at throwing those savage cross-blocks to break up a double play."

David King, a writer with diamondangle.com, went through Ross Youngs' files at the Baseball Hall of Fame in Cooperstown, New York, and found a few clippings and photos that provide a portrait of somebody who lived and played fast and hard, one of those people who made the world seem a little more energetic when they were in it. King wrote of Youngs:

Ross Youngs was one of the game's early stars from Texas and a favorite of John McGraw. *National Baseball Hall of Fame.*

He attacked second base with ferocious slides designed to break up double plays—and unnerve infielders. He attacked every form of competition, from football to basketball to golf. But baseball was his love, and the one he attacked with the most ferocity. And he played it for the most ferocious of managers, John McGraw—who took to him with the tenderness reserved for a son and guided him onto a journey toward greatness.

Ross Youngs was at the peak of his career when he came down with a kidney ailment, perhaps Bright's disease, and died in 1927 at the age of thirty. He was inducted into the Hall of Fame in 1972. Authors Lawrence Ritter and Donald Honig included him in their book *The 100 Greatest Baseball Players of All Time.* Other than that, Youngs' exploits have been all but forgotten, even in his home state, but John McGraw never forgot him. From 1927 on, McGraw always kept two pictures above his desk. One was of Christy Mathewson. The other was of Ross Youngs.

THE GREY EAGLE
AND RAJAH

One day, Tristram Speaker set out from his home near Hubbard with a penny in one hand and a Sunday school quarterly in the other. He returned that afternoon with neither the penny nor the quarterly, but he had a story to tell that explained his dirty and tattered appearance. "I beat 'em, Muvver!" he exclaimed. "I hit two home runs and a single! I made them and we beat!" Speaker's "muvver" chastened the boy and assured him he wouldn't beat anybody the next Sunday.

Tris Speaker's first passion was horses, and he took to riding them in a hell-bent-for-leather fashion and didn't necessarily bother with a saddle and bridle. His older sister, Pearl Speaker Scott, told interviewer Gordon Cobbledick that her little brother's fascination with fast horses caused some anxious moments in the Speaker house:

> I recall a time we missed him in the house and mother sent some of us girls to look for him. Pretty soon we saw a horse galloping down the road with a tiny kid in skirts perched way up on its back, digging his heels into the horse's ribs to make it go faster. We managed to flag the brute down and pull Tris off. Mother gave him a spanking and then the whole family practically fainted.

The family's fears were realized one day when Tris was thrown from a bucking bronco and suffered multiple fractures of his lower right arm and a clean break of his upper right arm and collarbone. Speaker had discovered

Tris Speaker was one of the greatest center fielders of all time. *Library of Congress.*

his passion for baseball by this time, and he figured his days as a ballplayer might be over before they really began.

A natural right-hander, Speaker began throwing with his left arm and found that he was actually more accurate with his left. Essentially ambidextrous, he took to batting from that side of the plate as well. Even years later, as the best center fielder in the Major Leagues, he sometimes astounded fans and players alike by catching and throwing the ball with the same hand. His sister wasn't surprised that Tris was good at baseball but rather that he stayed with it.

"Not that he wasn't always good at it, but baseball just seemed too tame to hold him long. Not enough excitement, you know," she said.

Speaker joined the Hubbard City town team when he was but a wee lad. Players from other teams would razz the Hubbard City nine about putting a mascot in the lineup, but they usually became more respectful of the mascot once the game began. From all accounts, Tris Speaker could play baseball better than anybody else almost from the first time he decided to give the game a try.

"All the ball fields around Hubbard City had skin diamonds, and the balls would get fuzzy after playing with them for a while," he said. "This would give pitchers a better chance to curve the ball, and the average player was handicapped, but it didn't seem to bother me." Tris's talent caught the attention of the North Texas League, one of two leagues struggling with each other and themselves to become the Texas League. League president J. Doak Roberts signed the eighteen-year-old lefty to play with a new team, the Cleburne Railroaders, in 1906.

The Railroaders lasted just that one year, but it was a memorable season. The Railroaders won the pennant, had a couple of no-hitters and played in the longest scoreless game in league history, a nineteen-inning affair that was eventually called because of darkness. It's worth noting that the game took only a little more than two hours to play. Speaker played right field in that game and caught the final out. He was signed by Cleburne as a pitcher, but this did not work out well; he lost his first seven starts. Still, at the plate and on the base paths, he was a marvel. He stole thirty-eight bases and hit .268, a respectable number in the dead ball era. It was hard not to notice that he was pretty handy with a glove, too.

A year later, playing for the Houston Buffs, Speaker led the league in hitting and would begin his Hall of Fame career in the big leagues with the Boston Red Sox the same year. He later played with the Cleveland Indians and finished his career with a .345 batting average, the fifth highest of all time, and still holds the record for most career doubles, with 792.

Nicknamed the "Grey Eagle" and "Spoke," he was the best center fielder of his era and many say the best center fielder ever. He played an extremely shallow center field, somewhat in the manner of a tenth player on a slow-pitch softball team today. He wasn't afraid to race backward for a long fly ball, but he could play a hard ground ball up the middle like an infielder.

His biographer, Tim Gay, said that on at least six occasions, and maybe as many as ten, he recorded an unassisted double play by racing in from center on a sinking line drive and beating the retreating runner back to the base. He used to throw runners out *at first base* from center field. All that is to say that he played baseball in the Major Leagues the same way he rode horses in Texas.

———

Rogers Hornsby was born in 1896 on a Hereford ranch near Winters, Texas, but after his father died when Rogers was two, the family moved to Fort Worth so his brothers could work in the meatpacking industry. We think of him as a sandlot player like Speaker, but Hornsby probably learned to play baseball in the city. He once said, "I can't remember anything that happened before I had a baseball in my hand." He played with the Swift and Company team when he was just ten years old and was playing semipro ball when he was fifteen. Three years later, he turned pro with Hugo in the

Texas-Oklahoma League for seventy-five dollars a month and later with the Denison Railroaders in Class D ball for ninety dollars.

When the St. Louis Cardinals played a series with the Railroaders during spring training in 1915, the Cardinals saw enough in the error-plagued, nineteen-year-old Class D infielder to buy his contract. The player who later would be called the greatest right-handed hitter ever was sold by the Railroaders to the Cardinals for $600. He played sparingly that first year and hit just .246 in fifty-seven plate appearances. Honus Wagner suggested that he set up deeper in the batter's box and step into any pitch that was over home plate. Hornsby hit .313 the next year. By 1922, he was the highest-paid player in National League history with a whopping salary of $18,500. He justified it by batting .401 and hitting forty-two home runs while striking out just fifty times. The next year, he hit .403 with thirty-nine home runs and the same number of strikeouts. He won seven batting titles in the 1920s and hit an astounding .424 in 1924, the highest any player has ever hit since 1900. His .358 average is second only to Ty Cobb on the all-time list.

Sportswriters dubbed him the "Rajah of Swat," which was eventually shortened to "Rajah." They called him the best right-handed hitter of all time. Hornsby meanwhile referred to his teammates as "humpty dumpties," "stool pigeons" and "sons of bitches." The Cards shipped him to the New York Giants in 1926, and the Giants sent him to the Boston Braves, who then unloaded him on the Chicago Cubs. The Cubs, perhaps used to suffering even then, put up with him for four years. He returned briefly to the Cards and then signed with the Browns in the American League, but that team fired him over a gambling scandal. Tris Speaker liked to ride horses; Hornsby liked to bet on them.

By the time Hornsby retired as a player, Major League Baseball wanted as little to do as possible with the greatest right-handed hitter ever. The Minneapolis Millers, a Double A team that trained in Daytona Beach, hired him as a coach. Ted Williams was a nineteen-year-old whiz kid on that team, and he always credited Hornsby with making him the hitter he was.

"I've always felt Rogers Hornsby was the greatest hitter for average and power in the history of baseball," Williams wrote in his book *My Turn at Bat*. "I liked Hornsby because he talked to me, a kid of nineteen, and boy I picked his brain for everything I could." Years later, after Williams won the Triple Crown, Hornsby referred to Ted Williams as "not a great hitter."

Hornsby was without parallel in his devotion to the holy game of baseball. He didn't read newspapers except for headlines, and he never went to movies

Rogers Hornsby had outstanding talent but a harsh personality. *Library of Congress.*

because he believed both activities hurt his batting eye. He couldn't read a racing form, but he bet on the ponies compulsively, usually with bad results; he was once sued by a bookie over a $70,000 gambling debt.

As a manager, he didn't like his players to stay at hotels with air conditioning because he believed that air conditioning "freezes up the body." He kept his players from swimming because he said swimming used the wrong muscles for baseball. Golf messed up the baseball swing.

"People ask me what I do in winter when there's no baseball. I'll tell you what I do: I stare out the window and wait for spring," he once said. Another time, he said that any able-bodied American boy who didn't play baseball was un-American. He quickly grew impatient with any conversation that centered on anything other than baseball; his own prowess was a particularly favorite subject.

Hornsby ended up back in Texas as a manager in the Texas League. He coached Oklahoma City in 1941 but resigned in June. He took over as skipper of the Fort Worth Cats the following year, 1942, which, because of World War II, was the last season the league played for three years. Hornsby returned to the Texas League in 1950 and led the Roughnecks to the league's best record.

Rogers Hornsby never changed his ways. He ate eggs for breakfast, steak for dinner and ice cream for dessert his entire adult life because he believed that protein kept his body strong. He died in January 1963 of heart failure at the age of sixty-six.

UNCLE BILLY, BIBB AND MR. RICKEY

The University of Texas (UT) and Texas A&M University first squared off on the baseball diamond long before they began their storied (and recently ended) football rivalry. In the early years of college baseball in Texas, any team that was in a conference with UT was expected to play for second place in that conference. The Longhorns were perennial champions in the Intercollegiate Athletic Association until 1909, when Texas Christian University took the title, and the following year, when academic scandal and a simply unacceptable losing record had some people suggesting that the Longhorns drop their baseball program.

Instead, the university hired Billy Disch from crosstown rival St. Edward's University in Austin to turn the program around. UT was familiar with Disch because his St. Ed's' teams played nearly .500 ball against the Longhorns when Disch was coaching them, despite UT always having far superior talent. Disch had played a little pro ball in the Texas League and in South Dakota. He came to Texas by way of Wisconsin, where he coached Sacred Heart College in Watertown. When the priest there was transferred to St. Edward's, Disch followed him to Austin. Disch's first UT team went 13-10-1 against college teams (13-12-1 overall), which was the closest thing to a losing season Billy Disch had at UT for the next twenty-nine years. The Southwest Conference was formed in 1915, and Disch's UT teams won fifteen of the first sixteen conference titles. Fans and sportswriters took to calling him "Uncle Billy."

Uncle Billy Disch established the baseball program at the University of Texas. *Portal to Texas History.*

Coming as he did from Catholic schools, Disch extended training rules and a strict code of conduct for his players. No drinking. No smoking. No chewing tobacco. No staying out late. No exceptions.

"I want no man on my team who hasn't the courage and the manliness to quit smoking cigarettes or any other kind of dissipation," he told the *Austin American-Statesman.* "I'd fire the most valuable player, if I knew that player was in violation of training rules, even though I had to play the mascot in his place."

Disch was so rigid that when a pitcher and first baseman named Bibb Augustus Falk reported to the Longhorns in 1918, Disch insisted on calling him Augustus because Bibb sounded to him like a frivolous nickname. Disch was not a frivolous man but he could spot talent, and Falk is a good example. Falk hit better than .400 each of his three seasons at UT and signed with the Chicago White Sox in 1920. The club offered to send him to the minor leagues, where he could play regularly, but Falk opted to stay with the parent club to get a taste of what major-league baseball was all about. The White Sox were considered the best team in baseball in 1920, despite a seemingly inexplicable loss to Cincinnati in the 1919 World Series that was explained later by revelations that certain Chicago players, including the popular Shoeless Joe Jackson, had conspired to throw the series.

When the Black Sox scandal broke in September and Shoeless Joe was among those banned from baseball for life, Bibb Falk replaced him in left field and hit .290 the rest of the season. Shoeless Joe's lost opportunity was Falk's open door to the big leagues, and he played with the White Sox from 1921 to 1928, hitting .345 in 1926. He retired with a .314 lifetime batting average and a .374 on-base percentage. He stayed in baseball, working alternately as a manager, coach and scout. When Billy Disch retired, he recommended Falk as his successor. Uncle Billy was

Bibb Falk took over in left field for Shoeless Joe Jackson and then took over for Billy Disch at UT. *Chuck Kaufman Collection.*

a tough coaching act to follow, but the UT baseball dynasty continued virtually unabated under Falk, winning another twenty Southwest Conference titles and two more national championships. Appropriately, the stadium where UT plays is named Disch-Falk Field.

In 1901, the National Association of Professional Baseball Leagues gave the minor leagues a structure that included the classifications ranging from the lowest rung of pro ball, Class D, to Triple A, one step away from the

Major Leagues. Minor-league ball flourished in every part of the state, just as semipro ball did. The Central Texas and Texas Association leagues of the 1910s and early 1920s were among the earlier leagues and featured the Marlin Bathers, the Mexia Gushers, the Terrell Terrors and the Palestine Pals. Austin, Corsicana, Sherman, Temple and Waco also fielded teams at various times.

In the early going, minor-league teams operated as independent clubs. A player might be bought in Houston or Corsicana and sold to a team in Milwaukee because the owners of the minor-league teams owned the players' contracts. San Antonio got Ike Boone, one of the best minor-league players ever, because New York Giants manager John McGraw was friends with San Antonio owner Harry Benson. Players came and players went, and so did managers and entire franchises. It was a freewheeling way to run a business and make a living. Branch Rickey saw an awful lot of talent either wasted or lost in the minor leagues.

Rickey was a catcher in the Texas League for a time, but his true calling was in the front office, where he made both subtle and monumental changes to the game over the next several decades. He was the first to rely heavily on statistics to judge talent and build teams. He hired Allan Roth to compile the stats, and Roth obliged, turning out numbers that astounded and baffled most people but which gave Rickey a new way of looking at baseball players as commodities to be bought, sold and traded. He even wrote an article about baseball statistics for *Life* magazine. The spread included pictures of the owlish Rickey standing in front of a chalkboard filled with complicated equations. Then, as now, the approach had its critics. "Doesn't he know what happened in the game?" John McGraw once growled when he saw Rickey keeping a detailed scorecard in the dugout.

As the general manager of a St. Louis team that was underfinanced and debt-ridden and thus could not afford to buy the best major-league talent, Rickey decided to corral as much of it as he could by buying minor-league teams and developing his own talent. The joke was that he was "growing players down on the farm like corn," and so it became known as the farm system.

Baseball commissioner Judge Kenesaw Mountain Landis opposed the farm system and did what he could to derail Rickey's plans. Rickey bought 19 percent of the Houston Buffaloes, who were owned at the time by a group of local businessmen headed by John Crooker. Rickey offered to sweeten the deal with a new $400,000 stadium about four miles east of downtown, conveniently located on streetcar and urban rail lines. From there, Rickey

Branch Rickey, owner of the Houston Buffs and other teams, created the farm system of minor-league baseball.

funneled as much minor-league talent as he could to Houston but kept the deal mum until the rules governing the relationship between the minors and Majors could be amended.

The new Houston stadium opened on April 11, 1928. Branch Rickey was there, and so was Landis, at Rickey's invitation. Landis was wined, dined and treated like royalty the whole time he was in Houston. The commissioner declared to the *Houston Post* that Buffs stadium was "the finest minor-league ball park in America."

Branch Rickey's 1928 Buffs finished in first place with a record of 104-54 and drew a record 186,469 people to the new ballpark. They beat the Wichita

HOFFMAN 2^{nd}B   STOW SS   PATE P   KRAFT 1^{st}B   MOORE C   WILLIAMS RF   HAWORTH C   ROBERTSON P

The 1920 Fort Worth Cats. A dynasty was in the making. *Mark and Pam Presswood Library Collection.*

Falls Spudders, who had matched the Buffs' win total, three games to one, to win the Texas League pennant and then knocked off the Birmingham Barons of the Southern Association to win the ninth annual Dixie Series, which pitted the champions of the Texas League against the champions of the Southern League.

The 1928 Houston team featured pitchers Tex Carleton, who grew up in Comanche, Texas, and lefty Wild Bill Hallahan, both of whom would go on to become crucial members of one of the most legendary baseball teams of all time: the fabled St. Louis Cardinals "Gashouse Gang" of the 1930s.

The true dynasty of the Texas League in the 1920s was the Fort Worth Panthers, nearly always called the Fort Worth Cats because it was a better fit for headlines. The Cats won every Texas League pennant from 1920 through 1925 and twice—in 1921 and 1924—won 109 games. Left-handed pitcher Joe Pate won 31 games. Twice.

The dynasty had its roots in a ruckus that Fort Worth owner H.N. Weaver unwittingly started when he stormed out of the stands to personally pull a struggling pitcher from the mound in the middle of a game, an act that humiliated the pitcher and embarrassed manager Jake Atz to the point that he resigned. Texas League president J. Walter Morris suggested that the Texas League would be better off without Weaver as an owner. Fort Worth businessman Will K. Stripling offered to buy the team, but only if a savvy baseball man was hired to run it. Morris suggested Paul LaGrave, a former teammate. Stripling agreed, and LaGrave promptly went about bringing Jake Atz back to Fort Worth.

Atz was born John Jacob Zimmerman in Washington, D.C., in 1879. He changed his name, he said, because in the army the soldiers were paid alphabetically, and he was always the last one to get paid. Or it was because he played on a lot of teams with financial problems, and they paid players alphabetically and ran out of money before they got to "Z." Atz was one of the first Jewish players in professional baseball and is believed to have been a vaudeville performer before turning to pro ball. He knocked around the lower echelons of the game with the Raleigh Senators and New Orleans Pelicans and played briefly with the Washington Senators before returning to

Top: Pitcher Joe Pate twice won thirty-one games in the Texas League. *Mark and Pam Presswood Library Collection.*

Bottom: Jake Atz was one of the first Jewish players in pro baseball and manger of the Fort Worth Cats. *Mark and Pam Presswood Library Collection.*

Paul LaGrave ran the Fort Worth Cats of the 1920s. *Mark and Pam Presswood Library Collection.*

the minors for several more seasons. In 1907, back with the Pelicans, Atz led the Southern Association with 158 hits.

The Chicago White Sox bought Atz's contract that year, and he played two seasons with Chicago, including 1909, when he was the starting second baseman. His career took a step back when Atz, taking one for the team, didn't step back from a Walter Johnson fastball and took it in the hip, causing him to walk with a limp for the rest of his life. He played a few more years in the minors and was hired in 1914 to manage the Panthers.

Aside from bringing Atz back, LaGrave's most significant signing was first baseman Clarence "Big Boy" Kraft, who, from 1918 through 1924, won a batting title and three home run titles and in 1924 drove in an astounding 196 runs, a record that still stands. He played three games with the Boston Braves in 1914 and went one for three. He never stepped up to the plate in the Major Leagues again, but he was a terror in the minor leagues.

When a livelier ball was introduced to the league in 1921, no one responded to the change with more enthusiasm than Big Boy Kraft, who hit eight home runs for Fort Worth in 1920 but clobbered thirty-one in 1921. Kraft continued to tear the cover off the new, livelier ball until he retired at age thirty-seven to take advantage of his name recognition in Fort Worth by opening an auto dealership. Kraft was part of Fort Worth's own "Murderer's Row," which included John "Ziggy" Sears, a perennial .300 hitter; big-league veteran Dugan Phelan; and slow-footed but hard-hitting Henry "Possum" Moore behind the plate, who got to handle one of the best ever minor-league pitching staffs.

Clarence "Big Boy" Kraft had just three major-league at-bats but was a terror in the Texas League. *Mark and Pam Presswood Library Collection.*

Joe Pate, with the two thirty-one-win seasons, was the ace of the staff, but there was also spitballer Paul Watchell, who won a league-record 231 games in the Texas League, and a right-hander, Lil Stoner, who pitched one year for the Cats (1923) and won 27 games before going on to enjoy a journeyman's career in the Major Leagues. Pate left for the Philadelphia A's; this, combined with Kraft's retirement and Stoner's promotion, gave the rest of the league a chance to catch up with the Cats.

LaGrave eventually became co-owner of the Cats with Stripling but contacted tuberculosis and died just prior to the season opener in 1929. Stripling sold the team, and the new owner fired Atz. The dynasty was over.

DIZZY DAZZLED

Some Texas leagues were professional in the sense that they paid people to play baseball for a team they ran. Usually, this was a large employer, like the meat companies that hired the Hornsby kids, including Rogers, to do a little work and play a little ball in exchange for regular paychecks.

After the turn of the century, some of the best paychecks came from the people with the most money, and after the discovery of oil—and lots of it—at Spindletop on January 10, 1901, many of those paychecks came from oil companies. The well at Spindletop was soon producing more oil than the rest of the world's wells combined, and it was only one of many oil fields in the state. The oil fields and the oil towns that sprung up alongside them were very good for baseball and for the millionaires and billionaires the oil industry created.

In 1923, a former scout and lease man for Standard Oil named Levi Smith became president of the newly formed Big Lake Oil Company and helped oversee development of the Big Lake oil field in west Texas, which included the Santa Rita No. 1 well owned by the University of Texas. Big Lake blossomed into a going enterprise with some 1,200 employees, and Smith built his own town, which he named Texon. Unlike other oil boomtowns he had seen, Texon offered grade schools, a church, a hospital, theaters, a golf course, tennis courts and a swimming pool.

Levi Smith was quite a baseball fan, too, and he sponsored a semipro team, the Texon Oilers, composed of company employees. Company employees played for the team along with current and former college

The 1926 Dallas Steers. *Mark and Pam Presswood Library Collection.*

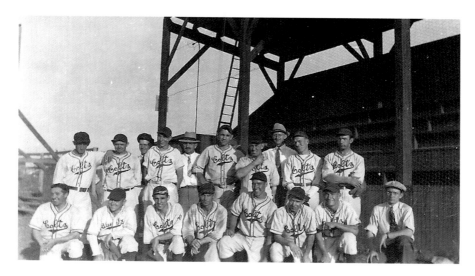

The 1928–29 Midland Colts. *Mark and Pam Presswood Library Collection.*

players and semipro players who needed jobs and whom Smith and others would hire for work and play. The Oilers played other west Texas teams from Big Lake, San Angelo, Alpine, Fort Stockton and Santa Rita. Then, as now, the teams that spent the most money on acquiring good players could usually be counted on to win the most games, and the Oilers were a prime example. They won the sixteen-state championship sponsored by a Denver newspaper and went on to win various titles in various leagues for the next several years.

The Oilers also played well-known Texas teams like the Fort Worth Cats and the House of David touring team from Michigan. The House of David team, longhaired and bearded, looks to us today more like a team from a 1960s commune or maybe the 1860s than like 1920s-era barnstormers. They represented the Israelite House of David commune in Benton Harbor, Michigan, and were one of the most popular barnstorming teams in the country during the 1920s and '30s. The House of David teams won a lot more games than they did converts, but they lost to the Texon Oilers in 1934, their first loss in two years. Notorious spitballer Snipe Conley, who won more than two hundred games in twelve years in the Texas League, managed the Texon Oilers from 1929 through 1932.

Texon won the All–West Texas pennant from 1933 through 1935 and the Permian Basin League championship in 1939, but the team disbanded during World War II. Snipe Conley tried to revive the team, but by the mid-'50s it was long gone—though it would be reborn, at least in spirit, with the Plymouth Oilers.

Oil companies weren't the only sponsors of amateur baseball in Texas during the early decades of the twentieth century. Business leagues and industrial leagues flourished in cities all across the state. The Employers Casualty Insurance Company of Dallas fielded a team in the 1920s and '30s that featured future major-league players Pinky Higgins, who played with the Red Sox and Tigers and ended his career as a scout for the Houston Colt .45s, and Dan Davenport, who played for the Chicago White Sox. The Employers team played against teams from Southwestern Bell Telephone, Baldwin Piano, Lone Star Gas Company and the U.S. Post Office. Many of the players were employees of the insurance company, including president and right fielder Austin Allen, but others were recruited to simply play ball. The company paid for all uniforms and equipment. The players practiced after work and played games on Saturdays.

Employers Casualty won the all-city championship in 1929 and then won the next playoff round to take the West Texas title as well. It played a team from Houston in a best two of three for the state championship and lost the first game, 4–1, but bounced back in the second game for a 7–0 win. Houston was leading the third game, 6–5, when the game was called on account of darkness. Employers Casualty protested, but to no avail.

The San Antonio Public Service Corporation also fielded a baseball team in the '20s. A representative of that company hired a lanky country kid from Arkansas named Jerome Dean, who was just out of the U.S. Army, as a meter reader in 1929. While Dean's talents as a meter reader have not been recorded, the fact that he could throw a baseball harder and straighter, except when he made it curve, than just about anybody is a matter of record. Pitching for a barracks team in San Antonio while he was in the army, Dean truly expected to receive a visit from a major-league scout any day, but it didn't happen. Instead, he got a visit from a representative of the San Antonio Public Service Corporation, who told him that the road to the Major Leagues ran through the minor leagues, with teams such as the one that the corporation fielded. Well, not *exactly* like that, since the team wasn't actually, you know, a *professional* team, and it didn't play in what might be called a professional league. But hey, he could get paid as a meter reader as part of the bargain! It was the best and only offer Dean got, so he took it.

A St. Louis Cardinals scout saw Dean pitch for the San Antonio team and alerted the front office that he had found a live one, a big ol' kid from Lucas, Arkansas, who threw smoke and wasn't signed by any other team. Dean signed with the Houston Buffs in May 1930, but the Cardinals sent him to St. Joseph in the Western League for a little seasoning. He went 17-8 with St. Joseph and was called back to Houston, where he finished 8-2. He pitched an exhibition game against the Chicago White Sox in which Mike Kelley, a Chicago coach who was disgusted with his hitters' efforts against Dean, told them, "That kid is making you look dizzy." Of course, that's one of several stories about how Jerome Dean became known as Dizzy Dean.

Dean made his major-league debut in 1930, on the last day of the season, after the pennant had already been decided. His foes, the Pittsburg Pirates, featured Paul and Honus Wagner and Pie Traynor, a trio of future hall of famers. Red Smith, then toiling as a sportswriter for the *St. Louis Star-Times*, was one of the first to publicly take note of Dean: "If a single performance in a single meaningless game can be taken as a criterion, then Dean is destined for stardom. The youngster showed burning speed, a wide, sweeping curve, a clever change, and best of all, unusual control for a rookie. You should know this young man."

Buoyed by the press clipping and brimming with self-confidence, Dean showed up to the 1931 spring training camp fully expecting to become a full-fledged member of the Cardinals. Rickey, owner Sam Breadon and most of the Cardinals had a hard time abiding Dean. They sent him back to Houston. "Don't you want to win the pennant this year?" he asked, astonished. Then he got on the train to Houston and pitched a three-hit shutout against the

Dizzy Dean thrilled Texas League fans while bedeviling managers and owners. *Answers.com.*

Wichita Falls Spudders that night. He then went on a tear like few leagues, minor or major, have ever seen.

At that time, in the throes of the Depression, some Texas League teams drew just a few hundred fans, but the Buffs averaged more than three thousand in 1931 when Ol' Diz was their star. Twelve thousand showed up

LaGrave Field in Fort Worth. *Portal to Texas History.*

for Dean's second appearance when he shut out Shreveport on four hits. He won five straight, got married and went on to compile a 26-10 record, with eleven shutouts and 303 strikeouts. They couldn't keep Dizzy Dean down on the farm after that. He started on his Hall of Fame career with the Cardinals the next year, winning thirty games in 1934.

Rube, Willie and Smokey Joe

It's a safe bet that no African American players were on the field when the Stonewall Jacksons and the Robert E. Lees squared off on that makeshift diamond at San Jacinto in 1867. With rare and only temporary exceptions, no African Americans took the field with white players for all of the nineteenth century and almost half of the twentieth. The gentleman's agreement that kept professional baseball segregated worked the same way on the amateur and recreational levels as well. African Americans took to baseball with zeal equal to or greater to that of white players, but they could only play with and usually against one another.

The first black teams formed much the same way the white teams did. Neighbors played neighbors, communities played other communities and neighborhoods took on other neighborhoods for bragging rights. In Houston, where baseball history always seems to begin in Texas, the Houston Postoffice Carriers formed one of the early organized teams. In Diboll, the players all worked for the Southern Pine Lumber Company but without any formal involvement of the company.

Newspaper accounts of those early days are sketchy. Players were often referred to by nicknames like "Tank," "Crush," "Coon" and "Sweetheart." As a result, their true identities have never been revealed, except perhaps in family histories.

Rube Foster was an outstanding pitcher and a key figure in the formation of professional Negro League baseball.

By the 1920s, black community newspapers began providing more detailed and formal descriptions of the games. A group of African American businessmen who sponsored various teams around the state made what turned out to be a halfhearted stab at forming the Texas Colored Baseball League in 1921. They came back the next year with a more austere business plan and a public relations campaign. The season opener against the Black Giants and Fort Worth Panthers was heralded with a parade and prominent press coverage, but sporadic attendance that could range from a few thousand to a few hundred to just a few eventually doomed the league, though local black semipro leagues continued to flourish in the 1920s and '30s.

Andrew "Rube" Foster was born in Calvert in 1879 and was pitching for the semipro Waco Yellow Jackets by the time he was seventeen. He was a right-hander, six feet, four inches tall and more than two hundred pounds with a blazing fastball and a "reverse curve" that broke left to right, the opposite of most breaking balls from right-handed pitchers. He supposedly got the nickname "Rube" from the time he was pitching for a semipro team in Hot Springs, Arkansas, and beat Philadelphia Athletics Hall of Fame pitcher Rube Waddell in an exhibition game.

In 1902, Foster met Frank Leland, who was one of the first to experiment with black baseball as a business. Foster pitched briefly for Leland's Chicago Union Giants and later for the Cuban X-Giants from Philadelphia, where he reportedly went an astounding 54-1. With Foster pitching most of the time, Philadelphia won three league championships in three years. The Giants were owned by a man named Sol White, who wrote the first book on African American baseball. *Sol White's Official Base Ball Guide* was first published in 1907 and contained a chapter written by Foster with advice on stretching, conditioning and "warming up" before pitching in earnest. He stressed the importance of good control and knowing when and where to throw certain pitches and at which times. It was a thinking man's guide to pitching—not simply throwing the ball toward home plate but doing so with a purpose and a strategy.

Foster returned to Chicago to play for Leland on what was now known as the Leland Giants. As player-manager, Foster employed a wide-open offense that must have dazzled and befuddled opponents. Foster's Giants used the hit-and-run whenever possible. No player was expected to stick around a base once he reached it. If a base was open, the runner was expected to steal it or get thrown out trying. If two were open, the time was right for a double steal. He pioneered the "bunt-and-run," sort of a sacrifice bunt on stimulants that was supposed to end up with the runner on first advancing all the way to third.

Foster brought the Giants to Texas in 1909 and 1910 on what were basically homecoming tours for him. He had left Texas as the most dominant pitcher in the state and returned as the most dominant figure in all of African American baseball. The *Indianapolis Freeman* reported that when Foster and the Giants went to Fort Worth, he was given "a welcome that would have done honor to the President of the United States."

Back in Chicago, Foster tried to strengthen his grip on African American baseball by removing competitors and generally taking on anybody who threatened to get in his way or questioned his authority and right to control everything he wanted to control, which was, well, everything that had anything to do with African American baseball. He feuded with other owners in public and quarreled with opposing managers, owners and umpires, with sometimes-riotous conclusions.

This went on for some time before Foster declared that, really, all of this feuding and raiding other teams for talent and badmouthing had to end. That much of this behavior had come from Foster himself didn't matter because Foster held up his end of the deal. In so doing, he helped create the Negro National League, which provided an opportunity for African American players to make a living playing a game that they loved every bit as much as did their white counterparts. Foster died at age forty-two in 1930, about the same time the Negro National League disbanded. He left behind a legacy as a player but also as the man who did the most to elevate black baseball from amateur to professional status.

———

Foster helped pave the way for other Negro League players, including several from Texas, like Smokey Joe Williams and Willie Wells. Foster tried to sign Wells to a contract with the American Giants when Wells was still a teenager, as did Bill Wallace with the St. Louis Stars. Wells's mother settled the matter by telling both men that her son, a graduate of Anderson High School in Austin, had no time to play professional baseball because he was going to attend college. When Foster and Wallace both promised that her son would be able to attend college in the off-season, she told Willie to sign with the Stars because St. Louis was closer to Austin than Chicago.

Nothing in Wells's rookie season foreshadowed the outstanding career he would have playing baseball. Like many otherwise promising prospects, Wells was baffled by professional curve balls. Players on the opposing team would start razzing Wells every time he came to the plate. "Hey, Wells, here comes the curve ball." Even though he covered more ground at shortstop than anybody else, he looked to be just another good-field, no-hit disappointment. Willie went back to Austin and enrolled at what is now Huston-Tillotson College, figuring his baseball career was already over, when he got a call to play winter ball in California. This time, Willie made up his own mind and went to California. He later recalled, "I looked at her [his mother] taking in washing and ironing. 'Now I can help her.'"

Wells got the help he needed in California. A man named Hurley "Bugger" McNair taught Wells to hit the curve ball by tying his ankle to a stake at home plate to keep him from bailing out on the pitch and then fed him nothing but curve balls. When Wells showed up for spring training and pitchers' eyes lit up when they saw him coming to the plate, he responded to their curve balls by smashing them all over and out of the park.

"He could hit to all fields, hit with power, bunt and stretch singles into doubles and doubles into triples," longtime Negro League player and

Willie Wells was one of the best shortstops to ever play the game, but not many people knew it.

manager Buck O'Neil said of Wells. "But it was his glove that truly dazzled…Old-timers in St. Louis who saw Willie play for the St. Louis Stars still have not seen his equal."

For a time, Wells played with fellow Texan Newt Allen at second base. Together they formed the best double-play combination in baseball. Former

Negro League player Bill Drake recalled that Allen wouldn't even look at first when he made the pivot at second on a double play. "He'd throw the ball to first under his left arm," Drake said.

———

Joe Williams was known as "Smokey Joe" and "Cyclone Joe" in the way that a future Texas fireballer, Nolan Ryan, would be known as the "Ryan Express." Like Ryan, Williams was the dominant pitcher in the game for as long as he stayed in it, which was a very long time. Asked how and when he learned to pitch, Williams once said, "Someone gave me a ball at a very early age, and it was my companion for a long time…I carried it in my pocket and slept with it under my pillow. I always wanted to be a pitcher."

After playing with semipro teams in San Antonio and Austin, Williams signed with the San Antonio Black Bronchos in 1905 and won nearly one hundred games over the next five years. Ross Youngs reportedly gave him the name "Smokey Joe" after the New York Giants faced Williams and his fastball in an exhibition.

Smokey Joe played briefly for the Birmingham Black Barons but returned to Texas because he was homesick. Signed by the Leland Giants in 1910, he caught the attention of teammates, fans, opposing hitters and Giants owner and namesake Frank Leland, who said of Williams, "If you have ever witnessed the speed of a pebble in a storm you have not seen the equal of the speed possessed by this wonder Texas Giant. He is the king of all pitchers hailing from the Lone Star State and you have to see him but once to exclaim, 'That's a plenty.'"

Pitching in the relative obscurity of the Negro Leagues, Williams was arguably the best pitcher in any of the black or white leagues. Like Ryan, he put up some truly astonishing numbers, such as a 41-3 record in 1914. Ty Cobb, a virulent racist but a man who knew good pitching when he saw it, allowed that Smokey Joe would have been a sure thirty-game winner in the Majors. Statistics are spotty, but Williams is on record as having outdueled such pitching legends as Walter Johnson, Grover Cleveland Alexander and Waite Hoite. Also like Ryan, Smokey Joe kept sending opposing hitters back to the dugout, bat in tow, well into his forties by adding change-ups and breaking pitches to his repertoire.

Williams pitched for twenty-seven years, from 1905 to 1932, in the Negro Leagues, in Mexico and the Caribbean. He struck out batters and won

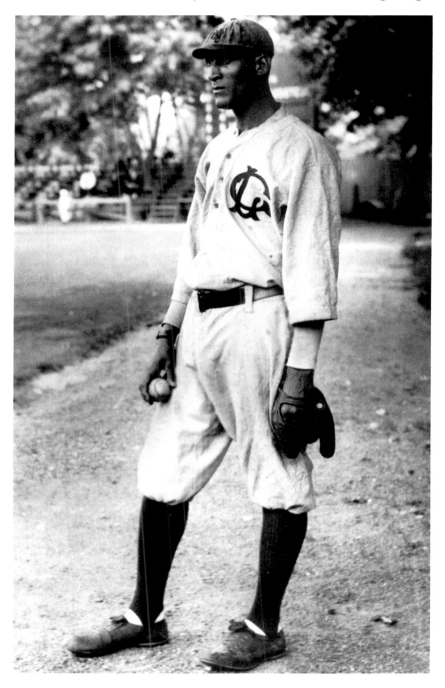

Joe Williams is considered, along with Satchel Paige, the most dominating pitcher from the Negro League era.

ball games everywhere he went. More than once he pitched both ends of a double-header and won both games. Once, he lost a 1–0 decision in the first game of a twin bill but pitched a no-hitter in the nightcap.

When the *Pittsburgh Courier* polled a group of former Negro League players and African American sportswriters to select a Negro League "dream team," Williams edged out Satchel Paige and Foster as the best pitcher the league ever saw. Williams pitched several years for the Homestead Grays in his late thirties and early forties, notching several more no-hitters and shutouts along the way.

Wells and Williams were just two of the outstanding players from Texas to star in the Negro Leagues. Andy Cooper was a star with the Kansas City Monarchs and Detroit Stars in the 1920s and 1930s. Catcher Lewis Santop, who played with the Fort Worth Wonders in the first decade of the twentieth century and on teams in Austin and San Antonio, was one of the great home run hitters of the era. Hilton Smith, from Giddings, won twenty or more games twelve times but was best known as Satchel Paige's relief pitcher. Paige was a big draw and started most of the games for the Kansas City Monarchs, but he'd often pitch just a couple of innings. In would come Hilton Smith from first base to finish the game. Smith was inducted into the Baseball Hall of Fame in 2001.

"What's Wrong with Negro Baseball?"

At age sixty-one, Branch Rickey, the man who brought the minor-league farm system to Major League Baseball, went to work for the Brooklyn Dodgers as a general manager. He had one more idea he wanted to implement: he wanted to integrate Major League Baseball. The player he chose to help achieve this was a multi-sport superstar from California named Jackie Robinson. Fleet Walker had played in the very early days, before Cap Anson refused to play on the same field as black players, and helped cement a gentleman's agreement that stayed in effect until Rickey disagreed and Robinson suffered the legendary slings and arrows of that first year to become a major star and trailblazer.

Jackie Robinson didn't spend much time in Texas, and much of the time he did spend there was not pleasant. He had joined the army in April 1942 and was accepted, after some resistance, into the Officers' Candidate School (OCS). The United States was engaged in a war on two distant fronts, where nothing less than the future of the world hung in the balance, during a period of American history that straddled Jim Crow segregation and full-scale integration.

Robinson was accepted into the OCS, but he was assigned to an all-black battalion at Fort Hood in central Texas. He was nursing an ankle he had injured while playing football at Pasadena Junior College in California and was riding to the base hospital when a bus driver ordered him to the back of the bus. The army had desegregated its bus lines, but the driver either didn't know or didn't care. When the bus reached its destination, the driver told

Jackie Robinson's time in Texas was not always pleasant. *Library of Congress.*

military police that Robinson had been causing trouble. Robinson was taken into custody and eventually court-martialed for insubordination, but he was acquitted, which was good news not only for Robinson but also for Branch Rickey a few years later. It's doubtful Rickey would have chosen someone burdened with a dishonorable discharge from the army during World War II to break baseball's color barrier.

Robinson served as athletic director at Sam Huston College (now Huston-Tillotson College) in Austin during the 1944–45 school year. The Kansas City Monarchs of the Negro League wrote him while he was in Austin, offering him a contract. He played a year for the Monarchs, but Robinson didn't much care for the baseball, the accommodations or the pay. He wrote an essay for *Ebony* magazine called "What's Wrong with Negro Baseball?" and later, in his biography *I Never Had It Made*, summed up his feelings on the league by saying, "For me, it turned out to be a pretty miserable way to make a buck."

Baseball was a pretty lousy way for a lot of African Americans to make a buck, at least in the United States. Some, like Willie Wells, played ball in Cuba and then started playing in Mexico in the winter when Mexican millionaire Jorge Pasqual stocked his team with several stars from black baseball in order to win the Mexican League championship.

Wells played for Vera Cruz in 1940 and 1941, hitting .345 the first year and .347 the next. Fans loved him. They called him "El Diablo" (the Devil) for the way he handled the shortstop position. He lived in an affluent neighborhood, was paid well and wasn't discriminated against because of the color of his skin.

"I've found freedom and democracy here, something I never found in the United States," he told the *Pittsburg Courier*. "I was branded a Negro in the United States and had to act accordingly. Everything I did, including playing ball, was regarded by my color. Well, here in Mexico I am a man. I can go as far in baseball as I am capable."

Wells, who is also widely credited with introducing the batting helmet to baseball and modifications to the glove, went pretty far with the game as it was. He played professionally for twenty-eight years and even got to team with his son, Willie Wells Jr., at second base for the only father-son double play combination in pro baseball history. He retired in 1954 with a .364 average against other black teams, .410 against major leaguers.

The Texas minor leagues integrated in 1951 when Cy Fausett, president of the Lamesa Lobos of the Class C West Texas–New Mexico League, signed twenty-three-year-old shortstop J.W. Wingate. Wingate started strong with a six-game hitting streak, but the hits stopped coming and Wingate was released.

Dave Hoskins was the first African American to play regularly in the Texas League. *Mark and Pam Presswood Library Collection.*

The Texas League integrated when Dave Hoskins signed with the Dallas Eagles, affiliated with the Cleveland Indians, in 1952. Hoskins had also integrated the Central League as an outfielder for Grand Rapids, where pitchers routinely threw at his head and often hit their target. He left professional baseball for a time and returned to the Negro Leagues, again with Grand Rapids, where pitchers continued to mistake his head for the strike zone. Recovering after yet another beaning, Hoskins decided to change his ways. "I was getting tired of having pitchers throw at me," he said later. "I made up my mind to start throwing at other guys."

Just as Rickey had chosen Jackie Robinson to break the color barrier in the Major Leagues because he had the right stuff to pull it off, Dallas Eagles owner Dick Burnett wanted someone of similarly stern stuff to be a pioneer in what would often be a hostile environment. Hoskins was up to the task, winning twenty-two games with an ERA of 2.12 while also hitting .328. He went on to have a couple good years with the Indians, but he hurt his arm in 1954 and spent the next five years in the minors, ending his career with Dallas and with Spokane in the Pacific Coast League.

Other Texas League teams soon followed Burnett's lead and began integrating their teams. Bill Greason broke in with Oklahoma City in July 1952. He threw hard but led the Texas League in walks in 1953 with 162. He appeared in three games for the St. Louis Cardinals and then played for five more years in the minor leagues, including two years with the Houston Buffs. The Fort Worth Cats signed Maury Wills in 1955, and he hit just .203, but he could run. He stole what was at the time a record 104 bases in 1962.

One of the last players from Texas to play in the Negro Leagues was Ernie Banks, who was born in 1931 in Dallas, where he was a football, basketball and track star at Booker T. Washington High School. In the summer, he played baseball for the Dallas Black Giants, and even when he was a teenager people were saying that Ernie Banks was the best shortstop anybody had seen since Willie Wells, who was just then hanging up his glove for good. As good a hitter as Wells was, Banks was even better. Just a flick of Banks's wrists, it seemed, sent baseballs on long journeys beyond outfield walls. When Wells was a teenager, the only scouts attending his games would have been from the Negro Leagues. Major-league scouts turned out in droves to see this Banks kid. The Chicago Cubs signed him in 1953; he never played for another team—and, consequently, never played in a World Series—but he was elected to the Hall of Fame in his first year of eligibility in 1976.

Ernie Banks, from Dallas, played for the Kansas City Monarchs before becoming "Mr. Cub" in Chicago.

Banks played a year for the Kansas City Monarchs and

then entered the military for two years. He was the first African American to play for the Cubs, and he broke in with them in 1953 without so much as a cup of coffee in the minor leagues. His career is the stuff of legends: 512 home runs, eleven all-star games and Most Valuable Player honors in 1958 and '59, making him the first player to win the MVP award two years in a row. Known as "Mr. Cub," Banks was a fan favorite. His saying, "Let's play two" became a catch phrase intended to express such delight in playing baseball that one game would simply not be enough.

The first African American player to be inudcted into the Baseball Hall of Fame was Frank Robinson,who was born in Beaumont in 1935 but moved to California at a young age. He hit 586 home runs in his twenty-year career and was the first African American to manage a major-league team, taking over the Cleveland Indians in the American League as a player-manager the last two years of his career and later managing the San Francisco Giants and Montreal Expos.

Oilers, Cowboys and Education through Recreation

World War II slowed down professional baseball but didn't bring it to a standstill, as had been the case in 1918, when the World Series was played in September. President Roosevelt gave baseball a "green light" to proceed with business as usual in 1942, and the Major Leagues carried on, without interruption, for the duration of the war. Baseball players weren't exempt from military obligations, and teams still had to cope with travel and materials shortages. Still, most teams did not suffer unduly. Most of the Major Leagues' highest-paid stars were already in the military, reducing their payroll. Attendance stayed fairly steady, and the play was good, though there weren't a lot of minor-league players to rely on for reserves. Most of the minor leagues shut down for at least a portion of the war, including the Texas League, which ceased operations from 1943 to 1945. By the end of the war, only ten minor leagues were still in operation. The Texas League resumed play after the war, as did most of the other minor leagues.

Semipro baseball continued to flourish in Texas, still fueled in many parts of the state by oil companies. The Plymouth Oil Company was a sister company of Big Lake and operated in south Texas on the Walder Ranch north of Sinton in San Patrico County.

Several former Texon Oilers working for Plymouth formed the Sinton Eagles, which played in the Coastal Bend Semi-Pro League. Mike Griffin, an executive with Plymouth Oil and a former business manager of the Texon Oilers, bought the Sinton team, built a ballpark at the Farm Labor Center south of Sinton and changed the name of the team to the Plymouth Oilers.

Griffin installed one-hundred-foot towers, each with twenty-four lights, at the Oilers field, and the team opened the 1950 season "under the lights" against the Houston Buffs of the Texas League. Night games weren't unheard of but were still a novelty, especially at the semipro level. The first time two major-league teams ever played a night game was on February 22, 1931, at Buffs Stadium in Houston when the Chicago White Sox and New York Giants squared off under the lights in an exhibition game. A regular season major-league game wouldn't be played under the lights for another five years.

The Oilers more than held their own in some fast company and often faced another Texas semipro powerhouse, the Alpine Cowboys, in the National Baseball Congress (NBC) Tournament in Wichita, Kansas. Mention an Oilers-Cowboys rivalry today and people might think you're talking about NFL football in the 1970s, but the Plymouth Oilers and the Alpine Cowboys emerged in the '50s as two of the best semipro teams in the country.

Alpine, located in a rugged isolated part of the state, started fielding a team in the early 1900s and played against other town teams—"town" being a relative term in those wide-open spaces—from Marfa, Fort Stockton, Pecos, Marathon and Sanderson. Other teams like the Alpine Vaqueros and Orient Team (named for the Orient Railroad) were formed, along with a Hispanic team known as the Alpine Internationals. Interest fell off during the Depression but returned stronger than ever in the 1940s and '50s.

Herbert Kokernot Jr., owner of the vast 06 Ranch and a baseball fan, had a stadium built for the Alpine Cowboys that was not only the equal of any minor-league park but was also better than some major-league facilities. It cost $1.25 million to build, or more than $1 million more than was spent to build Wrigley Field three decades earlier. Kokernot looked for the best players from the state and beyond and paid them for home runs, innings pitched and work they did on his 06 Ranch. College players from all over the country began spending their summers in Alpine, usually capped by a trip to the National Baseball Congress (NBC) championship tournament in Wichita, Kansas, where they were likely to encounter the Plymouth Oilers.

Like their Texon counterparts, and like Kokernot, Plymouth was always on the lookout for part- or full-time employees who could also play a little ball. Edward A. "Red" Borom was such a man. He had knocked around minor-league baseball for more than a decade and played briefly with the Detroit Tigers in 1944 and '45, but he went back to the minors when the major-league stars and starters returned home from the war. Borom came to Texas with his family and played a year for Tyler in the East Texas League and then for a semipro team in Mount Pleasant before signing on with the Plymouth Oilers in 1951. With a roster that included former major leaguers Tom McBride and Roy Easterwood, in addition to Borom, the '51 Oilers breezed through the regular season with a 55-11 record.

Both the Oilers and the Cowboys qualified for the National Baseball Congress championship tournament in Wichita, Kansas, in 1951, when the Oilers finished fourth and received a Sportsmanship Trophy. Oiler pitcher Pat Hubert, a student at Texas A&M University, threw the first no-hitter in NBC tournament history when he no-hit a Wyoming team in 1950.

Red Borom played in the Majors and minors and for the Plymouth Oilers.

The second no-hitter in tournament history came in '51, when the Oilers' Mike Blyzaka held a team from Camp Pickett, Virginia, hitless. The Oilers beat a team from Atwater, California, to become the first team from Texas to win the NBC championship.

The Oilers and the Cowboys tied for third at the 1956 tournament. In 1958, the NBC declared that Sinton, Texas, was the premier city in the nation, per capita, for promoting semipro baseball. That same year, the Plymouth Oil Company, citing economic reasons, discontinued its support of the Oilers, and the team disbanded.

The end of the decade was also the end of the line for semipro baseball in Alpine. Herbert Kokernot had put in lights at the best little ballpark in Texas in 1958, but the truth was that semipro baseball was dying, and no amount of money could change that fact. The army was no longer sponsoring service teams, and bad times in the oil business removed another group of sponsors. Teams like the Cowboys that hung on found they had nobody to play against.

Kokernot resisted offers to field a minor-league team until 1959, when the Boston Red Sox anointed Alpine the smallest town in the country with a minor-league baseball team by making it a Class D affiliate. The Red Sox allowed the team to keep its Cowboys name and to keep the outfield walls free of advertising—another unique feature. The league folded three years later, and Kokernot was not too upset about it. He never really cared to have a major-league team calling the shots for him.

As semipro baseball began to fall away from the landscape by the 1950s, another form of town ball, centered on the local high school and college teams, began to take its place. "Education through recreation" had become a rallying cry in certain parts of society, and physical education classes and sports teams were added to curriculums across the country. By the mid-1920s, nearly every state in the union had established athletic organizations of one kind or another to manage interscholastic competition. In Texas, that duty was handed to the University of Texas, which created the University Interscholastic League (UIL) to supervise and regulate sports on the secondary school level.

The first UIL-sanctioned Texas high school baseball state championship was played in 1949 and won by the El Paso Bowie Bears, a true rags-to-riches story in terms of recognition if not actual riches. Located in El Paso's poverty-ravaged second ward, Bowie didn't field a team until 1946.

Coach William Carson "Nemo" Herrera, who coached high school sports for eighteen years at San Antonio Lanier and had played a few years of semipro ball, was hired to coach the new Bowie team. Herrera quickly put together a team that played aggressive, fundamental baseball. They ran the bases and fielded their positions, and the pitchers threw strikes. Players who didn't do those things were replaced by players who did. To sharpen their skills, Herrera scheduled games against military teams from Fort Bliss and Biggers Field. Aside from the competition, the kids were allowed to eat at the mess hall. Usually, it was the only meal they would have all day.

Bowie beat El Paso High for the district championship and went on the road to play the bi-district round in Lamesa, where the appearance of so many Hispanic teenagers made the team a center of not-always-friendly attention; many of their Anglo counterparts seemed overly concerned that the Bears might have somehow forgotten about the Alamo. The Bears won the best-of-three series against Lamesa and went to Austin for the UIL's first eight-team, single-elimination tournament. Austin, Beaumont, Denison, Lubbock, Marshall, Stephenville and Waco were the other teams. The other six teams that traveled to Austin for the tournament checked into hotels, but the Bears slept on cots under the stands at Memorial Stadium, UT's football field, and walked across the field to the field house to use the bathroom.

None of this seemed to bother the Bowie team, which knocked off Stephenville in the first round and outlasted Waco in a twelve-inning thriller in the semifinals. That put the Bears in the championship game against Austin High, which had not only beaten every high school team it played but also defeated the University of Texas freshman team. Austin's ace, Jack Brinkely, was destined for the Boston Braves. Bowie's ace, Trini Guillen, was battling strep throat and had already thrown a lot of innings. Herrera went with Lefty Holquin as the starter in the championship game. Holquin had a knuckleball that his teammates couldn't catch, and it was reasoned that Austin hitters wouldn't be able to hit it, either.

The reasoning seemed correct through the first three innings. When Herrera pulled Holquin in favor of Guillen in the fourth, it was because he had walked a couple of batters. Bowie was up 1–0 at this point and extended the lead to 3–0 going into the seventh and final inning. Austin rallied for two runs, but Guillen closed the door, and the Bears returned to a hero's welcome in El Paso with the state's first high school baseball trophy in tow.

The UIL stayed with the eight-team, single-elimination format for deciding a champion until 1957, when the championship was divided into two divisions: 4A for big schools and 3A for the smaller schools. In this format, four teams from two divisions played for the championship in their division. The losers of the first two games played each other for third place. Abilene won the first 4A championship, and Bryan was the first 3A champ. In the 1960s, Houston Bellaire, under Ray Knoblauch, and Lubbock Monterey, under Bobby Moegle, came to dominate the larger division. Both programs continued for decades under the same mentors. Moegle is second on the national list of most wins by a high school baseball coach, with 1,114.

The University of Texas continued to dominate college baseball in the state, even after Bibb Falk stepped down and the reins were handed to Cliff Gustafson. Gustafson grew up outside Kenedy, Texas, the son of a cotton farmer who died when Cliff was five, leaving him and his brother, Marvin, to pick the family's cotton crop by themselves. When Cliff was in his early teens, his mother moved the family to San Antonio, where he quickly made himself at home on the basketball court, football field and baseball diamond.

He played for Falk in 1952, on one of Falk's championship teams, making him one of the few to both play and coach in the College World Series.

Gustafson tried his hand at pro ball with Plainview in the Class B Texas–New Mexico League but quit to take a coaching job at South San Antonio High School, which won seven state championships while Gustafson was there. His record at South San Antonio was 344-85-5. When UT football coach and athletic director Darrell Royal called Gustafson to offer him the job at UT, Gustafson hung up on him. He thought it was a prank. His fellow Southwest Conference coaches had many occasions to wish it had been. Under Gustafson, the Longhorns went to the College World Series a record seventeen times, winning national championship in 1975 and 1983.

Battling a Slump

The caliber of play in both the Majors and minors was at an all-time high in the 1950s, partly because of integration and also because generations of young Americans had grown up with the game. Some of the greatest superstars the game has ever seen—such as Hank Aaron, Willie Mays, Mickey Mantle and others—were ratcheting up the level of play on the field. Competition for a spot on a big-league roster was more difficult than ever as African American players and foreign-born players from countries like Venezuela and Cuba were coming to the United States to play in the most competitive and highest-paying league.

This was happening at a time when the sport itself was mired in a long economic slump. Attendance at major-league ballparks dropped dramatically to just 17,227,000 in 1950 and 2,000,000 fewer than that in 1952. The minor leagues were hit especially hard as attendance plummeted and leagues shut down for good, especially in the small towns. In a lot of the big cities, neighborhoods where the ballparks were located had decayed and deteriorated into areas of high crime. More and more games were being played at night, and a country that was dispersing from the cities to the suburbs had less and less to do with the cities, and that included attending their baseball games. If they wanted to watch baseball, they could turn on their TVs on Saturdays and watch the game of the week. In 1950, about 25 percent of Americans owned televisions. By the end of the decade, nearly 85 percent of the homes in America had TVs.

The 1947 Waco Dons. *Mark and Pam Presswood Library Collection.*

The 1950s-era Abilene Blue Sox. *Mark and Pam Pam Presswood Library Collection.*

This was about the time that Dick Burnett bought the Dallas franchise, in 1948, reportedly paying several times what the team was worth. He spent a quarter of a million dollars building a new stadium, which he decided should be called Burnett Stadium. He was by all accounts a fiery individual who was known to throw typewriters from the press box and castigate his own players from behind the backstop. He wanted to bring a big-league team to Texas, and he saw owning the Dallas franchise as a necessary first step.

For opening day in 1950, Burnett determined that Dallas should break the single-game attendance record, which was held by Fort Worth, with 16,018, in 1930, and he rented out the Cotton Bowl, with a capacity of more than 75,000, to play the game. Burnett's gimmick for getting people to pack the stadium was to suit up an all-star cast of former players for the Dallas Eagles to square off against one Tulsa batter.

For their part, the old-timers were reluctant to take part in Burnett's scheme until sixty-three-year-old Ty Cobb agreed to play. Others included Charlie Gehringer, Frank "Home Run" Baker, Travis Jackson, Mickey Cochrane, Tris Speaker and Dizzy Dean. All but two of the players Burnett lined up for the game are in the Hall of Fame.

The game was heavily publicized in the weeks leading up to it. The players were recognized with a parade through downtown Dallas, and 54,151 paid to see the game, though it was reported that many of the fans left after the old-timers took batting practice and that Ty Cobb yanked a few into the stands just to show that he still could. Ol' Diz walked the first and only batter he faced and then got into a scripted rhubarb with the umpire, who ejected him. The rest of the old-timers took their leave, and Burnett had his team in the record books for drawing the most people ever to a Texas League game.

Other minor leagues battled the drop in attendance while also presenting high-quality baseball to the fans. Out in arid and windy west Texas, where a long drive to center can suddenly turn foul, professional leagues got a foothold with the West Texas League, the West Texas–New Mexico League and the Longhorn League. There was no such thing as a pitcher-friendly park in these leagues, but hitters often found those prevailing and gusty west Texas winds to be one of the best performance enhancers ever.

Joe Baumann, playing for the Roswell Rockets in 1954, hit 72 home runs, a pro baseball record that stood until Barry Bonds broke it in 2001. Baumann never made it to the big leagues, despite 337 career home runs and a .337 lifetime average.

The 1947 Lubbock Hubbers, so named because of Lubbock's designation as the Hub City of the South Plains, won ninety-nine games in 1947,

OFFICIAL SCORE CARD

LUBBOCK

HUBBERS

VS.

EL PASO

TEXANS

FREE

West Texas - New Mexico League

Not just a good deal, but a Great deal....

On a new

WOMBLE OLDS

1955 Oldsmobile

at

Womble Olds

1211-19th

Lubbock Hubbers scorecard from 1955. *Mark and Pam Presswood Library Collection.*

averaging almost nine runs a game; six Hubbers scored one hundred or more runs. The undisputed star of the team was shortstop Bill Serena, who at five feet, nine inches and 180 pounds wasn't as big as most epic sluggers, but he hit fifty-seven regular season home runs and then clouted thirteen more in a fifteen-game playoff run, giving him seventy for the season. Serena played five years for the Chicago Cubs, but a fractured wrist cut short his playing career. He was a major-league scout for thirty-two years, including twenty-five with the Braves.

In east Texas, as in west Texas, oil fueled many of the local economies in the early decades of the twentieth century, and the team names reflected that. Several teams were named Oilers, and you also had Nitros, Boomers, Drillers, Gassers and Gushers. Several leagues that stated in east Texas played in an East Texas League, which would occasionally morph into a Lone Star, Dixie or Dixie West League. The Big State League lasted from 1947 to 1957 and featured teams from Austin, Gainesville, Greenville, Sherman-Dennison, Temple, Texarkana and Wichita Falls. Teams operated off and on in the Rio Grande Valley for many years, but the Rio Grande Valley League later became part of the Gulf Coast League.

These were the days when players like Baumann played their entire careers in the minor leagues. If they were "good enough to dream," as Roger Kahn so eloquently put it, they stayed with the game they loved until they were too

TOP ROW L-R Bob Conwell, Bus. Mgr., Fred Smith, Fred Bell, Bob Mover, Gene Wulf, Hugh King, Lionel Campbell, President
SECOND ROW L-R Salty Parker, Lem Pillar, Dale Myrland, Lon Goldstein, Ev Hall, Don Spyker, Bill McClain
FRONT ROW L-R Milton Carver, Ken Jones, Dutch Schroeder, Zip Zunno, Jerry Kaires, Bill Turk, Mike Goldstein

Above: The 1952 Temple Eagles. *Mark and Pam Presswood Library Collection.*

Right: Eddie Knoblauch was a lifetime minor-league player, and a good one. *Mark and Pam Presswood Library Collection.*

old to play at any professional level. Even then, the smart ones got out of the game before their skills totally eroded.

Eddie Knoblauch was one of the smart ones, and one of the good ones, too. He played for sixteen years in the minor leagues, including eleven in the Texas League, and finished his career with 2,543 hits and 1,420 runs scored. Knoblauch scored 125 times in the one season he played for the Kilgore Boomers in the East Texas League, and he hit .308 for the Houston Buffs in 1942 before spending 1943–45 in the military during World War II. He returned to Houston after the war and played for Shreveport, Tulsa, Dallas and Beaumont, hitting better than .300 eight times. Teammates used to say of him that he could hit .300 whenever the hell he wanted to. He was never under contract to a major-league team and seemed to prefer it that way. Knoblauch concluded his career in 1955 at the age of thirty-seven. He started the season with Beaumont but was traded to the Dallas Eagles early in the season and finished with a .327 average to win his first Texas League batting title in his final season.

Eddie's brother Ray Knoblauch pitched in the minor leagues for a decade, going 84-81. He was 20-7 with a 3.06 ERA with the Odessa Oilers, but he was wild; he struck out 162 batters in 226 innings but walked 148 and led the league in wild pitches. After he stepped away from the game, he became a teacher and baseball coach at Bellaire High School in Houston, leading the school to four state titles. Ray Knoblauch turned out a slew of future major leaguers, including Jim Gideon, Kelly Wunsch, Jose Cruz Jr. and his son, Chuck Knoblauch, who played college ball at Texas A&M University and spent eleven years in the Major Leagues.

BIG-LEAGUE DREAMS

The Houston Buffs left the Texas League for the American Association as an independent team when that league expanded in 1959. Managed by former major leaguer Rube Walker, the Buffs managed to lose more than 100 games—104 to be exact—while winning just 58. They became affiliated with the Chicago Cubs the following year and were managed by Enos Slaughter, who inserted himself into a few games and managed to hit .289 at the tail end of his Hall of Fame career. A couple other future members of the Hall of Fame, outfielder Billy Williams and third baseman Ron Santo, were on the field for the Buffs that year. Grady Hatton, Lou Klein, Fred Martin and Harry Craft all took turns managing.

There was talk, and there had been for some time, that Houston was a major-league city and deserved its own major-league baseball team. Pushing to bring baseball to Houston was the Houston Sports Association, which consisted of Houston businessmen George Kirksey, a former UPI baseball writer; Craig Cullinan Jr.; Judge Roy Hofheinz; R.E. Smith; and K.S. (Bud) Adams, who would later own the Houston Oilers and Tennessee Titans football teams. The association tried to buy existing franchises in Philadelphia, Cleveland and St. Louis, but to no avail. Fortunately for Houston, Branch Rickey was still around.

In 1959, at the age of seventy-eight, Rickey threw himself into the promotion of a third major league that would exploit not only a second team in the huge New York market but also teams in Houston, Dallas, Atlanta, Denver and other cities. Rickey and his associates dreamed up the

The 1940 Houston Buffs. Houston was an early and avid supporter of baseball in Texas.

Continental League of Professional Baseball teams and announced that the league would begin play in 1961.

The American and National League owners moved quickly to squelch the deal, agreeing to New York's return to the National League and moving the Washington franchise to Minneapolis–St. Paul. A new team, the Angels, owned by cowboy singer and actor Gene Autry, set up shop in Los Angeles, across town from the Dodgers. The Senators continued in Washington, causing some confusion since the Minnesota Twins (the first team to be named after an entire state) were actually the previous year's Washington Senators, while the 1961 Senators were completely new. In the rush to expand, the Continental League died quietly, never to be heard from again.

Kirksey was executive vice-president of the Houston Sports Association and its spokesman. When the National League awarded Houston a franchise, Kirksey hired Gabe Paul as general manager to take care of the nitty-gritty business of selecting front office personnel, scouts, free agents and players and organizing a minor league, along with hundreds of other details that had to be taken care of before a team could be put on the field. Speaking of which, the new team also needed a place to play.

Gabe Paul seemed well on his way to bringing Houston into the big leagues when he suddenly and quite unexpectedly announced that he was leaving Houston to accept a similar post at Cleveland. "I am leaving Houston for personal reasons," he said. "I have a good opportunity in Cleveland and believe it too good to pass up." That was the last Houston heard from Gabe Paul.

Kirksey hired Paul Richards to replace Paul. Richards was a native Texan, born in Waxahachie and called the "Wizard of Waxahachie" as a successful big-league manager. Richards started out as a pitcher and earned a bit of notoriety when, playing for the Muskogee Chiefs of the Class C Western Association, he pitched an inning using both hands. He pitched right-handed to right-handed hitters and switched to his left hand when a left-handed hitter stepped to the plate. Facing a switch-hitter, Richards switched from one hand to the other. He eventually switched to catcher and played seven years in the minor leagues before making his major-league debut with the Brooklyn Dodgers in 1932. Richards bounced back and forth from the minors to the Majors until he was forty, when he retired as a player and became manager of the Chicago White Sox in 1951. He moved to Baltimore and was the Orioles' field manager and general manager through 1958, the first man to hold both positions simultaneously since John McGraw. He served strictly as the Orioles' field manager until 1960, when he left to become the general manager in Houston.

Bobby Bragan making the tag at home in a Texas League game. *Mark and Pam Presswood Library Collection.*

Bobby Bragan became president of the Texas League in 1969. *Mark and Pam Presswood Library Collection.*

Had Gabe Paul stayed on as Houston's general manager, Alabama-born Bobby Bragan would likely have been the Colt .45s' first manager. Bragan played in the Major Leagues for eight years, starting as a shortstop for the Philadelphia Phillies. Later, he became backup catcher for the Brooklyn Dodgers, and it was for that team and in that capacity that he ended his major-league playing career. Rickey and Bragan clashed over the Jackie Robinson issue, but Rickey saw something in Bragan and hired him to manage the Fort Worth Cats, now a farm team of the Dodgers. For his part, Bragan said early and often that he was wrong to oppose Robinson.

As manager of the Cats, Bragan was an immediate success, his fortunes boosted no doubt by the presence of future major-league stars like Carl Erskine. Fort Worth won the Texas League pennant with Bragan serving as manager and catcher in 1948 and won one hundred games in 1949. The Cats set a Texas League record for the most victories on the road, partly because a fire burned LaGrave Field, where the Cats played their home games. They carried on a bit amid the charred ruins, but many of their home games were home games in name only that year.

Bragan managed in the Major Leagues for several years, but he could never duplicate the success he had at Fort Worth. Cleveland general manager Frank Lane fired Bragan, telling him, "Bobby, I don't know how we're going to get along without you, but starting tomorrow, we're going to try." Bragan returned to Texas and became president of the Texas League in 1969 and served in that capacity through 1975.

Instead of Bragan, Richards went with Harry Craft, who had the reputation of being able to work with young players. Craft, a center fielder with Cincinnati in the 1930s and early 1940s, had managed the Kansas City Athletics and was in Houston when the Buffs moved to the American Association. The new New York team, named the Mets, stocked its initial roster with aging veterans. Houston determined to go with young players whom they would develop in the minor leagues, and Craft was deemed to be the man for the job.

With key people in place, location became the next major issue. Voters in Harris County approved a $20 million bond issue for a domed stadium, complete with air conditioning, to be ready for play in 1962, but legal squabbles slowed progress, and plans had to be made quickly for a temporary park on land adjacent to where the domed stadium would be built.

A "Name the Team" contest resulted in the team being named the Houston Colt .45s in honor of the "gun that won the West" and not, as some surmised, for a popular malt liquor of the same name. The first uniforms featured a gun with a wisp of smoke spelling "Colts" across the chest of the home jerseys. Navy blue and orange were the colors. The stadium-in-waiting was named Colt Stadium and seated thirty-three thousand, with one tier of multicolored seats and bleachers extending from the right field foul pole to home plate, all the way to the foul pole in left field, with more seats in right and left field. The scoreboard was part of the center field wall.

The first major-league team in Texas, the 1962 Houston Colt .45s. *Houston Astros.*

Colt Stadium goes down in history as the hottest place in the world to play a baseball game. During one Sunday doubleheader, more than one hundred fans were sent to the first-aid room. Mosquitoes that plagued the park were described, maybe with some exaggeration, as being the size of hummingbirds.

As for who would play in Colt Stadium, the National League asked each of the present eight teams to file a list in September 1961 of 15 players; 7 players would come from the major-league club, along with 8 minor leaguers and players with options currently under contract for that major-league team. In this way, each team put 15 players into the expansion draft, giving Houston and New York 120 players to choose from.

The two teams then chose two players from each of the eight teams for $75,000 apiece. If they wanted a third player from a team, they had to pay another $50,000. Also, one player from each team's list of fifteen was listed as a "premium" player and could be had for $125,000, but since neither Houston nor New York could take more than one premium player per team, they had four premium selections for an overall cost of $500,000. Houston took pitcher Dick "Turk" Farrell, catcher and utility man Hal Smith, infielder Joe Amalfitano and outfielder Al Spangler as its premium selections and the nucleus of the new team.

Houston also took third baseman Bob Aspromonte, shortstop Bob Lillis and outfielder Roman Mejias, as well as pitchers Ken Johnson, Jim Golden and Bobby Shantz. While New York went with older, more recognizable names like Gil Hodges for its initial team, Richards and Director of Personnel Bragan chose to build for the future. By the time the domed stadium was built, the thinking went, they would have a team worthy of such a venue.

Bob Aspromonte was a fan favorite for the Colt .45s. *Houston Astros.*

The team that assembled in Apache Junction, Arizona, for its first spring training was a group of mostly young players who saw this as a real shot to play in the Major Leagues, and they responded with enthusiasm. Apache Junction was Geronimo's old stomping grounds and a base of operations for him and his band of warriors. Some locals said that training in the shadow of Superstition Mountain, where old Apache spirits and the ghost of an old Dutchman were said to guard a lost mine, was bad luck. Maybe. Maybe not. The team won seventeen of its twenty-eight exhibition games, but in the season opener, outfielder Al Heist stepped in a hole and broke his ankle.

Opening day on April 10, 1962, at Colt Stadium against the Chicago Cubs was cold, windy and threatening rain. The Mets' first game had already been rained out, giving Houston the national spotlight to itself. Shantz, a wily little southpaw, was the Colt .45s' opening-day pitcher. His first pitch was a strike, but many of the 25,271 fans who bought tickets were stuck in traffic along South Main or trying to get into one of the parking lot entrances, so they missed the first major-league pitch in Houston history. The first run came when Aspromonte led off with a single and Spangler tripled him home. Shantz pitched a complete-game five-hitter in an 11–2 Houston win. Mejias, whom the Colts picked up from Pittsburgh, hit two home runs, continuing a torrid pace he had started in spring training. The Cubs got one of their two runs on Ernie Banks's home run in the seventh.

Hal Woodeschick and Farrell combined to shut out the Cubs, 2–0, the next night. Dean Stone followed that with a three-hit shutout the following night in another 2–0 win. For three days in April, it looked like these upstart Colt .45s were going to run away with the pennant.

By the time Houston got a major-league team, generations of boys had grown up in Texas wanting to play in the Major Leagues. For most of that time, games were played in sandlots, vacant lots and cow pastures all over the state and country. After World War II, a lot of these kids had fewer chores to do than the previous generation, and fewer of them had to take jobs to make ends meet. They had nothing to do all day in the summer except play baseball, and they did. Most didn't have the talent to play professionally, but they had the time to become the best players they could be and to dream big-league dreams in those vacant lots and cow pastures. Every boy of a certain age in America, it seems, grew up wanting to be a major-league baseball player. Many a big-league dream was born on those sandlots, and most of them stayed there.

Nolan Ryan was one of those kids who grew up with sandlot baseball and who also played Little League baseball. Of the two, Ryan credited the sandlot games for doing the most to hone his skills. He remembered those early days in his autobiography, *Miracle Man: Nolan Ryan*:

> *In the summertime there was always a baseball game, and all we'd do is play ball. It was horribly hot and humid, but we didn't care until sometimes in the middle of the day when it was so hot you couldn't stand out in the sun. Then we'd lie around in the shade until it cooled down a few degrees and we could get back at it…You get used to the ball. Your brain recorded angles and bounces and hops and even sounds. There's something about hitting a hundred different times in a day-long game, about throwing and fielding and running. You've got to wonder if today's kid could play that much.*

Some scouts thought Ryan was too skinny and too wild to be a prospect. One of those who paid the closest attention was Red Murff, who had been around Texas and professional baseball for most of his life. Murff was a veteran of the Texas League and a star in the minors, but he wasn't called up to the Major Leagues until 1956, when he was thirty-five years old. The year before, pitching for the Dallas Eagles, he went 27-11 and was named the *Sporting News* Minor League Player of the Year. When the Milwaukee Braves offered to buy Murff's contract from the Eagles, Murff played owner Dick Burnett to determine the exact terms of the trade—or at least that's the way Murff told it. The Braves ended up buying Murff's contract for $40,000.

Murff had just been to a Houston Astros game where Houston's Dick Farrell and Jim Malone of Cincinnati, two of the hardest throwers in baseball, hooked up in a pitching duel. Murff stopped off at a high school tournament that evening and got his first glimpse of Nolan Ryan's fastball. He pigeonholed Alvin coach Jim Watson after the game and asked, "Who the hell was that kid?" Murff made it a point to be at as many of Alvin's games as he could after that. "I saw two great arms that day," Murff later recalled. "Then I saw this skinny kid throwing better."

Ryan signed with the Mets in the eighth round of the 1965 draft, the 295th overall pick. He signed the contract and then headed out to Marion, Virginia, home of the Mets' Class A affiliate. He was miserable and lonely for his girlfriend, Ruth Holdorff (soon to become Ruth Ryan), but he struck out 115 batters in seventy-eight innings. Still, not many people in Texas paid much attention to what some gangly kid from Alvin was doing in the Mets farm system. They had their own big-league team to follow.

———

Texas was enthusiastic about its first major-league team, at least for a while. For a lot of them, the radio broadcasts of Gene Elston and Loel Passe were their link to the Houston Colt .45s and to Major League Baseball. Elston was smooth and polished, the guy who would always let you know the score, the inning and who was up next. Passe had a bag of phrases that he would pull out at appropriate times, like "Now you chunking in there!" which was meant to let the listener know that a pitcher was throwing strikes. Passe usually added the name of the pitcher, as in, "Now you chunking in there, *Turk Farrell*!" Others included: "He *breezed* him one more time," meaning the pitcher struck the batter out. He had others like "Hot ziggedy dog and ol' sassafras tea!" and "Chain me to the chair!" meant to convey the extreme excitement of the moment. He liked to say, "Now you going in there, Colt .45s!" whenever the team rallied or scored.

What didn't come across on the radio was how plain miserable playing at Colt Stadium was. The heat and the mosquitoes were the main complaints, especially from umpires, who hated pulling duty in this new major-league city, where it was too hot to even breathe right and where sweat stung your eyes and, yes, sometimes made it hard to see. Generally a hardy breed, several men in blue had to be treated for heat prostration at Colt Stadium.

Players complained that the lights weren't very good. Outfielders complained about the outfield. Infielders complained about the infield. Pitchers complained about the mound. Batters swore there were "blind spots" during the pitcher's delivery. Everybody complained about the mosquitoes. By the time summer rolled around, there was time to complain about the play on the field as well, but there were a couple of bright spots, and they were named Farrell and Mejias.

Farrell managed to lose twenty games in the team's inaugural season, but he had one of the best earned run averages (ERA) in the league: 3.02. He was just one of four pitchers to strike out more than 200 batters (203), but finished with a 10-20 record.

The Colts went thirty-eight innings without scoring a run in a four-game series against the Reds, breaking the old record of twenty-eight innings set by the 1904 New York Giants.

Ken Johnson had the worst luck. He went 7-16 in 1962 but with a decent 3.84 ERA. His 2.65 ERA the next year was better than Dodger ace Don Drysdale, who won twenty-five games, but Johnson's record was just 11-17. Johnson's hard-luck woes reached a peak on April 24, 1964, when he played his former team, the Cincinnati Reds, who had exposed him to the expansion draft. It was a good news, bad news kind of game. Johnson spun a no-hitter but was on the wrong end of a 1–0 score when the Reds managed an unearned run in the ninth.

After the game, Pete Runnels tried to console Johnson. "Someone pitches a no-hitter every year," he said. "Yours, though, people will remember."

You Can't Lose 'Em All

Most of the Colt .45s' actual firepower that year came from Roman Mejias, an affable, good-natured player from Abreus, Cuba, whose demeanor, humility and enthusiasm reminded some people of Ernie Banks. Mejias was working in the sugar cane fields when he was signed to the Pirates by George Sisler, the Hall of Famer who was now scouting for Pittsburgh. Mejias played for Waco in the Class B Big State League, where he hit safely in fifty-four consecutive games and finished with a .354 batting average. The Pirates brought him up to the big leagues, but the Pirates' outfield of Bob Skinner, Bill Virdon and Roberto Clemente was one of the best in baseball.

The Pirates, hard-pressed to get Mejias in the lineup, made him available in the expansion draft, and Houston grabbed him for $75,000. He tore up Cactus League pitching and continued his torrid streak into the first half of the season. He hit safely in each of the Colt .45s' first eight games, a franchise record that has been tied (by Jeff Keppinger in 2009) but never surpassed. He kept up his pace through the first half of the season but was not named to the all-star team, a snub that reportedly bothered him. He battled injuries in the second half of the season, and his production fell off, but he finished with a .286 average, twenty-four home runs and seventy-six RBIs. In what would be a trend for Houston, one that has continued, the team traded Mejias the next year.

The Colt .45s lost ninety-six games that first year and, despite the lack of ambience at Colt Stadium, drew almost a million fans. Houston won their

Roman Mejias went from the sugar cane fields of Cuba to the Pittsburgh Pirates to the Colt .45s, where he had the best years of his career. *Houston Astros.*

season series against the Mets and the Cubs but couldn't win so much as a single game against the Philadelphia Phillies. Houston, buoyed by a stellar pitching staff that sparkled whenever the .45s scored runs, slipped into eighth place ahead of the Cubs and Mets in late August. That brought the Phillies, winners of fifteen straight against Houston, to Colt Stadium for a three-game series highlighted by a Labor Day double-header.

With the Colt .45s surging, Houston officials decided it was time to "break the jinx" against the Phillies. Surely, the reasoning went, Houston's lack of success was due to bad luck. Maybe it went back to their spring training camp on the happy hunting grounds of the former Apache warriors, but bad luck was a persistent theme of the first-year Colt .45s. To break the jinx and perhaps drum up some karma for the home team, Houston Sports Association vice-president George Kirksey hired a former boxer named Young Kid Dugan to put the Slobtke Stare and the Transcontinental Eye on the Phillies. It didn't work. The Phillies were impervious to Dugan's evil eye and all the alternate good luck charms and hexes he aligned against them. The Phillies swept the Colts, 3–2 and 5–3, in a double-header. Fans called for Kid Dugan's head.

Bob Bruce, relying on nothing more than a baffling curve ball and excellent control, led Houston to a 4–1 win in the final game of the series.

Craft quipped, "You can't lose 'em all."

The Colts finished with a ninth-place record of 66-96 in 1963, thirty-three games behind the first-place Los Angeles Dodgers. Still, the team had its moments.

One of the best was provided by Bob Aspromonte, a crowd favorite and especially popular with youngsters. He also seemed to have a direct pipeline to the cosmos. In 1962, a boy by the name of Billy Bradley was struck by lightning and blinded during a Little League practice in El Dorado, Arkansas. He was sent to Houston for medical treatment, and Aspromonte, like a true Lone Star version of Babe Ruth, went to visit the child in the hospital. Bradley asked Aspromonte to hit a home run for him. Aspromonte said he'd try. The Babe was legendary for making that kind of promise to sick children, but Ruth had 714 home runs in his career, including 60 in the 1927 season. Aspromonte hit exactly 60 home runs in his entire thirteen-year career, including the one he yanked out of Colt Stadium that night for Billy Bradley.

Little Billy Bradley visited Houston for treatment twice more in 1963, and each time Aspromonte promised he would hit a home run for him. Not only did Aspromonte follow up on the promise both times, but *both home runs were grand slams*.

Unable to calculate the odds of such a thing happening, baseball fans threw up their hands and declared it to be a divine miracle.

Otherwise, miracles were hard to come by. Fans started turning their eyes to Houston's minor-league system and were encouraged by what they saw there. Of particular interest were the San Antonio Bullets, the Colts' Double A affiliate in the Texas League. Joe Morgan, at second base, held special interest. Morgan grew up in Oakland and was signed by Houston in 1963. He finished his first season of pro ball with a .310 average and eighteen home runs.

In 1964, Morgan was promoted to the Bullets, where he and shortstop Sonny Jackson formed the best double-play combination in the league. The Bullets led the league in twin killings, with 150. Morgan was nothing short of astonishing. He hit .323 with eight triples, twelve home runs and ninety RBIs.

The San Antonio Bullets represented what was happening in the minor leagues during this time as well as anybody. The play on the field was outstanding, with future Hall of Famers and future big-league stars scattered all over the diamond. Still, the people stayed away in droves. The Bullets drew just a little more than one thousand fans a game that year.

The Colt .45s put the team and fabled Mission Stadium up for sale. Richards blamed the local media for not covering the team more and reporting on the high level of play at Mission Stadium. He moved the

Joe Morgan and Sonny Jackson played together in the Texas League and were featured on the cover of *Sports Illustrated* with the Colt .45s.

team to Amarillo the following year; baseball was never played at Mission Stadium again. Even after baseball returned to San Antonio three years later, the Houston owners would not lease the stadium. The San Antonio Sports Association refurbished V.J. Keefe Field on the St. Mary's University campus for the new team, while Mission Stadium was left to rot and decay until it was torn down in 1974.

The emphasis on young players had yet to pay dividends for the Colt .45s, and that apparently led to some dissension in the front office ranks. The Colts had fielded a team composed of nothing but rookies for one game in September—anything to drum up interest in a struggling team, right?—but Craft wanted to put more experienced players into the mix. He was fired, and coach Luman Harris was hired to take his place.

One of the players the Houston front office wanted to see on the field was pitcher Larry Dierker, and they weren't necessarily inclined to wait until he grew up. They put him on the mound for his major-league debut on his eighteenth birthday, September 22, 1964, against the San Francisco Giants. He struck out Willie Mays in the first inning. Dierker went on to lose the

Larry Dierker in the spring of 1965. *Houston Astros.*

game, but he would be a fixture for Houston, in several capacities, for many years to come.

Born in Hollywood, California, in 1946, Dierker came up through Little League and was signed out of high school, a trend that had developed as high schools added baseball to their sports programs. He had offers from eighteen of the Major Leagues' twenty teams and signed with Houston because he felt he had a better chance to make the big leagues sooner there than he would with other teams. He was right. Dierker pitched a handful of innings in the Florida Instructional League and was called up to the big leagues to make his major-league debut on his birthday. Dierker was through with the minor leagues.

And Houston was through with old Colt Stadium. Apparently, it takes a while to finance and build something that can be called the "Eighth Wonder of the World," but in 1965, after three years in much-maligned Colt Stadium, the Astrodome was ready for its unveiling.

Dome Sweet Dome

People in Texas took note when, in 1939, air-conditioning pioneer Willis Carrier said the day would come when men would live under domes of transparent material, which would remove weather as a factor in work and play. Most people said Carrier was crazy, but among the people who thought he was on to something was Roy Hofheinz, who planned to air condition a shopping mall before he bought his way into Major League Baseball with the Houston Sports Association. Carrier was a man to listen to because he helped give the world air conditioning, and Hofheinz and others believed that Houston never would have grown by such leaps and bounds if its millions of citizens couldn't spend as much time as possible in an air-conditioned environment.

Prior to getting into the sports business with the Houston Sports Association, Hofheinz had been a state representative, a county judge and a controversial but popular mayor. In a city and state known for its larger-than-life characters, Hofheinz was another. Steve Rushin, writing in the August 16, 1994 issue of *Sports Illustrated*, described Hofheinz this way:

> *The Judge smoked 25 cigars a day, great tobacco-filled dirigibles that befit a man of his dimensions: the 57-inch waistline, the cuff links as big and loud as cymbals, the long Cadillac limousine in which he drove himself through Houston. It was said that Judge Roy Hofheinz could not find a chauffeur willing to work his hours, which were roughly the same as a 7-Eleven's.*

The Astrodome, "Eighth Wonder of the World."

Officially but rarely called the Harris County Dome Stadium, the Astrodome was the first domed, air-conditioned multipurpose sports stadium in the world and the prototype of the many domed stadiums dotting the sports landscape today. Love or loathe them, the Astrodome spawned them all.

Hofheinz's idea for a domed stadium called for $22 million through a general obligation bond issue, which voters approved. Voters then had to approve another bond issue of $9 million in December 1962 because building a domed stadium was more expensive than Hofheinz had figured. By the time it was done, the dome cost more than $40 million to build, and its primary occupant, the baseball team, was still battling to get out of last place.

Hofheinz decided that the Old West name of the Colt .45s was no longer appropriate, not in a thriving metropolis like Houston, which was also home to NASA and a focal point in the race to get to the moon. By the time the Astrodome opened, America was sending manned flights into space, and a moon landing was in NASA's sights. Hofheinz called up astronaut Alan Shepherd to ask if NASA would mind if he named his baseball team for them: the Astronauts. Shepherd didn't mind, and Hofheinz renamed the team but shortened it to Astros because he knew fans and headline writers would do the same thing anyway.

The jerseys changed. The gun was gone, and so was the word Colts, replaced by Astros. The caps at first had just a simple orange "H" on a navy background, but a white "H" with an orange star replaced it and lasted for more than thirty years, even as the uniforms went through some dramatic changes.

Larry Dierker, in the big leagues for good, arrived with the team in Houston from spring training in Florida in April 1965. The dome was lit up "like a birthday cake," he said. He and his teammates checked out their new digs and didn't quite know what to think. The air conditioner was on; they didn't know that the air conditioning *had* to be on or else it would rain. Grass was growing indoors, and the roof was translucent, giving the whole place the feel of a giant greenhouse. "It was," Dierker said, "like walking into the next century."

In this case, it turned out to be a case of one step forward, two steps back. The translucent roof created a glare that made fielding high-fly balls nearly impossible on extremely bright days, leaving some wags to wonder if games were going to be cancelled on account of sunshine. The first major-league game played at the Astrodome, an exhibition between the Houston Astros and the New York Yankees, was on April 9, 1965.

New York Yankees manager Johnny Keane batted Mickey Mantle leadoff so that Mantle could be the first player to bat in the Astrodome. Farrell was on the mound for the Colts. He gave up a single to Mantle during that quasi-historic first at-bat—it was, after all, an exhibition game—but he settled in after that, though Mantle hit one of his patented tape-measure home runs in the sixth inning. The Astros won in extra innings on a base hit by veteran second baseman Nellie Fox, who was keeping the position warm while Joe Morgan rounded into Hall of Fame form.

The first official game in the Astrodome was on April 12, 1965. The Phillies shut out the Astros, 2–0, on an opposite field home run by Richie Allen. The team responded to the stadium's glaring problem by painting over the translucent roof panels. That helped fielders track fly balls, but it killed the Tifway 419 Bermuda grass practically overnight. This wasn't completely unexpected. Hofheinz had suspected grass wouldn't thrive or even grow indoors, and he had been talking to people at Monsanto about a new artificial turf they were working on. Hofheinz showed enough interest that Monsanto named the stuff Astroturf and allowed Hofheinz to test it out to his heart's content. The dead grass and dirt in the Astrodome were painted over, mixed with sawdust and deemed playable. The stadium featured the newest technology, but the field, for that one year, wasn't much different from the sandlots. Astroturf was installed the next year. It worked so well that by 1973, seven teams had replaced their grass with it. The earliest version of Astroturf could be as hard as concrete, something the Houston Oilers football team, which also made the dome its home, experienced much more keenly than the Astros.

In September 1963, the Colt .45s had called up Joe Morgan from the minors for a peek at the big leagues, just to see how he handled himself on the larger stage. During that stint, he delivered a game-winning single against the Philadelphia Phillies, who were involved in a serious pennant race, and needed that game against the league's ninth-place team. In a now-famous rant after the game, Mauch chided his players for "getting beat by a guy who looks like a Little Leaguer."

Two years later, following his year at San Antonio, he was brought to the big leagues for good and quickly established team records with 601 at-bats, one hundred runs scored, 163 hits and twelve triples. For good measure, he added twenty-two doubles, twenty stolen bases and brilliant defensive play. All of this was good enough to earn him National League Rookie of the Year honors.

Former Bullets teammate Jim Wynn was in center field for the Astros and clubbed twenty-two home runs and drove in seventy-three runs while playing half his games in the pitcher-friendly confines of the Astrodome, where home runs went to die. For a power hitter, Wynn wasn't that much bigger than Little Joe. He was listed at five feet, ten inches and 170 pounds, but he used a cumbersome thirty-six-inch, thirty-six-ounce bat, and when he got hold of one he could hit a ball out of any park in the country, including Yellowstone.

Right fielder Rusty Staub, signed as a teenager by Houston in 1961, had been up and down ever since making his major-league debut in '62 while he was still a teenager. In '65, he began to come into his own, hitting .256 and fourteen home runs. None of this translated into a better record for the Astros, who finished at 65-97, thirty-two games behind the first-place Los Angeles Dodgers.

The Astros, under new manager Grady Hatton, seemed to be putting it all together—youth seemed on the verge of finally being served in Houston—in 1966. Morgan and Jackson were featured on the cover of *Sports Illustrated*, and Morgan was named to the all-star team, but the

JIM
WYNN
HOUSTON ASTROS   OUTFIELD

Jim Wynn established early records for home runs with Houston.

season quickly deteriorated. Morgan broke his kneecap, and Wynn's
season ended when he dislocated his elbow running into the center field
wall in Philadelphia. The team finished only slightly better than it had
before, with an eighth-place record of 72-90.

By 1968, none of the Astros' starting pitchers had a record better than .500; Don Wilson had the best winning percentage, with a 13-16 record. One highlight: Wilson and Tom Seaver hooked up in a classic pitching duel in a game that went twenty-four innings. Seaver pitched ten innings and gave up two hits while Wilson allowed five hits over nine innings. The game finally ended when Aspromonte drove in the winning run in the twenty-fourth. The Astros won seventy-two games but finished in last place in the National League, despite good numbers from Staub, Wynn and others.

By the end of the decade, the Astros were finally showing life on the field. The team's ascent in the standings in 1969 coincided with some unpopular moves that saw longtime favorite Aspromonte (who was often referred to as Aspro the Astro) traded to the Giants, where he joined Sonny Jackson in the infield. Rusty Staub went to the expansion team Montreal Expos. Promising pitcher Mike Cuellar was traded to the Baltimore Orioles, where he shared the Cy Young award with Denny McClain and fashioned a series of twenty-win seasons after that.

Still, there was hope. Wilson and Dierker led an improved pitching staff, with Wilson tossing his second no-hitter in May. Houston got hot early and stayed hot, and in September he was in fourth place but only two games out of first when they faced Atlanta in a crucial series. Larry Dierker pitched brilliantly but received little help at the plate from his teammate, and the game seeped into extra innings before the Astros scored a pair of runs in the thirteenth. Aspromonte and Jackson then led a three-run comeback by the Braves that seemed to take the steam out of the Astros.

The league's other 1962 expansion team, the Mets, much more woeful in the beginning and which had never finished higher than ninth, clawed and scrapped all the way to the World Series in 1969, aided in part by that hard-throwing right-hander from Alvin, Nolan Ryan.

Ryan pitched in twenty-five games for the Mets in that championship season, striking out 92 in 89.1 innings, while going 6-3 with a 3.53 ERA. He pitched 7.0 innings of relief against the Braves in the National League Championship Series and got his first playoff win in the process. He got a save in the '69 Series, with 2.1 innings of shutout relief against the Orioles, part of a five-game series victory for the Mets. Ryan never felt truly part of that team, and his 17-25 record over the next two years, even with 241 strikeouts, didn't inspire confidence in either the Mets or Ryan. He was traded to the Los Angeles Angels in December 1971.

Spec Richards took over as Houston general manager in 1967, and his name comes up often when people talk about the early-day Astros. And why not? He was the man who had traded Staub to the Montreal Expos for Donn Clendenon and Jesus Alou. Clendenon refused to report, and the Astros got $100,000 instead, but they lost Staub, who went on to have an outstanding

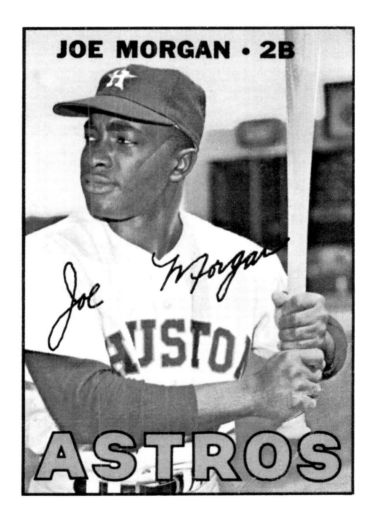

Joe Morgan was a standout with Houston until he was traded to Cincinnati, where he became a superstar.

career wearing other uniforms. On November 29, 1971, a day that lives in infamy for Astro fans, Richardson traded Joe Morgan to the Cincinnati Reds. Not only is it considered the worst trade in Houston baseball history, but it's also considered one of the worst trades in *baseball* history, right up there with Boston swapping Babe Ruth to the Yankees.

Morgan was simply stupendous at Cincinnati, scoring more than 100 runs six times and finishing with 286 career home runs. The Reds went on to win four divisional titles and two world championships over the next five years, and the Astros remained mired in mediocrity. In 1975, they were last in the National League, with a 64-97 record. That was the same year that the Reds won the first of two world championships and Morgan won the first of two MVP awards.

Joe Morgan would be elected to the Hall of Fame in 1990. Baseball writer and guru Bill James determined that, based on Morgan's value to a team and his production in all phases of the game over the course of his career, he is the best second baseman of all time. Rogers Hornsby, one of the best hitters ever with a .358 lifetime batting average, was ranked third.

BORN UNDER A BAD SIGN

I t's been said that the Texas Rangers baseball team was born under a bad sign, and nothing in the last days of the Washington Senators or the early days of the Rangers would seem to disprove that. The team that eventually became the Rangers had its start in 1961, the same year that Major League Baseball expanded to Houston, as the Washington Senators.

Actually, this was the second Washington Senators team. The first Senators team had a rich history and boasted Hall of Fame pitcher Walter Johnson, Lefty Gomez, George Sisler and Joe Cronin as alumni. Tris Speaker, the kid from Hubbard who went on to compile the lifetime .345 average, played his next-to-last season with the Senators at age thirty-nine. Johnson pitched for Washington his whole career and won 416 games, second on the all-time list. His career record for strikeouts—3,508—was one of those numbers that baseball people believed would never be eclipsed. That original team moved to Minnesota in 1961 and became the Minnesota Twins.

The Senators started out in last place, and for most of their time in D.C., they stayed there, giving rise to the slogan: "Washington, first in war, first in peace, and last place in the American League." The play *Damn Yankees* centered on a fan who sold his soul to the devil in exchange for the Senators winning the pennant. The play was a smash hit, partly because most people believed that was the only way the Senators would ever play in a World Series. The Senators lost more than one hundred games in each of their first four years. In 1965, bolstered by the acquisition of six-foot-seven, 250-pound slugger Frank Howard, Washington improved to 70-92. In the end, even Ted Williams, who was called on to manage the Senators, couldn't save the team from itself.

Ten days before the end of the 1971 season, Senators owner Bob Short announced he was moving the team to Texas. The last game the Senators would ever play in Washington came on the last day of September in front of 14,460 fans, many of them carrying anti-Short banners and signs. People hollered for Short to show his ugly face and other terms of endearment, but he was back home in Minnesota listening to the game on the radio. It had been decided, probably wisely, that attending the game might be hazardous to his health.

The home team fell behind to the damn Yankees, 5–1, in the sixth but clawed back, partly on the strength of Frank Howard's twenty-sixth home run of the season, and had a 7–5 lead going into the eighth. That's when things started getting weird as various mobs gathered in right field and along the baselines. With two outs in the ninth, hundreds of fans stormed the field, eager to take some part of RFK Stadium home with them as a souvenir. Others were clearly there to simply raise some hell and disrupt the game, which they did. Umpires and security had zero chance of controlling the crowd, and the game was forfeited to the Yankees.

Shirley Popovich, in one of his classic columns for the *Washington Post* the next day, wrote:

> *Those who were savoring this last, fond look at the Senators let it be known by their cheers that they absolved the athletes of all blame in the messy machinations that rooked the city of its major-league status. Even the .190 hitters heard the hearty farewells, and in the case of big Frank Howard it was thunderous when he came to the plate…If there was no general wet-eyed melancholia in the stadium, there were still unmistakable pockets of bitterness. From the upper stands hung banners spelling out four-letter words in large design, all of them reviling club owner Bob Short for shanghaiing the team to Texas…As if in sudden awareness that the end of major-league baseball in Washington was only one inning way, the mood hardened. "We want Bob Short!" was the cry that picked up in loud and angry chorus, and it was the baying-fury sound of a lynch mob.*

Former St. Louis Cardinals center fielder Curt Flood, who was born in Houston and reared in Oakland, California, tried to get back into baseball with the 1971 Senators. Curt Flood was a fleet-footed, all-star center fielder and .300 hitter with the St. Louis Cardinals in the mid-1960s when he, Tim McCarver and two other players were traded to the Philadelphia Phillies for Richie Allen. Flood resented having no say in where he was legally allowed to ply his trade and brought suit in the federal courts, arguing that the reserve clause violated his right to make a choice of where he worked. "I do not believe I am a piece of property to be bought and sold irrespective of my wishes," he wrote to baseball commissioner Bowie Kuhn. He sat out a year while the case made its way through the courts; he signed with the Senators the next year but played in only thirteen games before retiring.

The Supreme Court, citing two previous rulings that upheld the reserve clause, upheld it again in Flood's case. Flood and the players' union had lost the battle and, it seemed, the war, but that was not the case. Flood's challenge reverberated with players and with Marvin Miller and the Major League Baseball Players' Association. The clause was finally abolished by baseball in 1975, ushering in the era of free agency. Curt Flood, off the field, did more to change the business of baseball than anybody since Branch Rickey.

Big-league baseball players were restless as the decade began. A handful of players made more than $100,000, which was enough to make most people believe that baseball players were well taken care of by their teams and had no reason for unions and strikes. They weren't coal miners or longshoremen. The players went on strike after owners refused a 25 percent increase in the pension fund and improvements in medical benefits. Following executive director Marvin Miller's counsel, the Major League Baseball Players' Association (MLBPA) walked out of spring training camps.

In mid-April, the owners put $500,000 in the pension fund, and the players rejoined their clubs and started the season without a new basic agreement. The next year, the minimum salary would be increased to $16,500, along with a provision that allowed players with ten years of major-league service and five years with the same club to veto trades. Owners also agreed to accept binding arbitration in contract disputes with players having at least two years in the Majors.

At the time, it didn't seem like such a big deal.

After waiting ten days for the '72 season to open, the Texas Rangers played their first game on the road against the Anaheim Angels. Pitcher Dick Bosman carried a shutout into the ninth inning, but he got no run support, a familiar theme for pitchers with expansion teams in those days, and Texas lost 1–0 on a wild pitch in the bottom of the ninth. They beat the Angels, 5–1, the next day for their first victory, the first of fifty-four against one hundred losses.

The Rangers' leading home run hitter was Ted Ford with fourteen. Rich Hand was the leading pitcher with a 10-14 record. The only legend in the clubhouse was manager Ted Williams, who had been named Manager of the Year when the Senators clawed out of the cellar and almost into contention.

"Teddy Ballgame," as they called him, is widely regarded as the best hitter to ever play the game. He was the last player to hit .400, hitting .406 in 1941.

Williams wasn't crazy about his 1972 team, and he wasn't crazy about the heat at Arlington Stadium. If he was crazy at all, it was *because* of the team and the heat. He also drove some of the players crazy. A former catcher for the Rangers from 1972 to 1974, Dick Billings told *Texas Monthly* magazine that Williams would sometimes mumble words that he had not heard before. "He liked the barbecue and the fishing," Billings said. "That was about it."

Williams would tell his players to do things that he could do but that other human beings could not do, like hit the top of the baseball early in the game and the bottom of the

Top: Ted Williams was one of the greatest hitters of all time, but he never really connected as manager of the Texas Rangers.

Bottom: Whitey Herzog thought the Rangers hired him to nurture the team's young talent, but apparently he was wrong about that. *Texas Rangers.*

baseball late in the game. Ted Williams probably had the best eyesight of any player to ever play the game, and there is little doubt that he could actually choose which part of a ninety-mile-per-hour fastball to hit as it traveled his way from sixty feet, six inches away. Short was reluctant to fire a living legend, but Williams made it easy for him by quitting. Short surprised everyone by bringing in Whitey Herzog to manage the team.

Herzog brought an attitude and candor to the team that would keep him in good stead throughout an illustrious managerial career. Herzog had been a mediocre player who said his claim to fame as a player was that he once hit into an all-Cuban triple play: Camilio Pascual to Jose Valdivelso to Julio Becquer. He had played with the original Washington Senators and as a utility player for Casey Stengel's Yankees. "Baseball has been awfully good to me once I stopped trying to play it," he liked to say. He spent seven years as the New York Mets' director of player personnel, which coincided with that team's rise from the league's worst team to World Series champions. He was widely figured to be the Mets' next manager after Gil Hodges died just prior to the '72 season, but Yogi Berra, the team's first base coach, got the job instead. Herzog took the Rangers job.

Herzog never pretended he hadn't agreed to take over a team that had lost one hundred games the year before, and he never tried to tell sportswriters, fans or his team that he expected them to challenge anybody for a pennant in 1973. Clearly, he had demonstrated a knack for spotting and developing talent, and that was just what Short and the Ranger brain trust said they wanted. It was going to take some time, but Herzog was the perfect candidate. He had some talent to work with in future all-stars Toby Harrah, Jeff Burroughs and Bill Madlock, and he had some dependable veterans like Tom Grieve, a holdover from the Senators. His assessment: "Defensively, these guys are really substandard, but with our pitching it really doesn't matter."

For the second year in a row, the season opener went off with a hitch. This time it was a freak April snowstorm. In *Seasons in Hell*, Mike Shropshire wrote, "To Whitey Herzog, that amounted to a stay of execution. Well into August, Herzog could be seen in his office before games, praying for snow." Bosman, a twelve-year veteran in the twilight of his career, could still summon a masterpiece on the mound from time to time, as he had done on the delayed opening day a year earlier. This time he gave up a monstrous blast to Dick Allen while the Rangers scratched out four singles in a token show of support. The Rangers were off but not exactly running.

Meanwhile, the fans stayed away in droves. The problem that Short faced as owner was perhaps best summed up by Yogi Berra, who said, "If people don't want to come to the ballpark, no one is going to stop them." No one was stopping fans in the Metroplex from staying away, unless you counted the wildly popular Dallas Cowboys and even the high school football teams; some of the local Friday night high school games outdrew the Rangers.

Short's stated intentions might have been to bring the team along slowly with players Herzog and other key personnel would develop, but the problems in owning a team to which fans didn't cotton were acute and immediate. He had to do something, as he put it, to put some butts in the seats. From 1969, when he bought the team, through 1971, Short estimated his losses at $2.6 million. Short had put his break-even point in 1972 at 800,000 fans; the Rangers drew a little more than 620,000.

Short fell back on the same kinds of gimmicks and "special" nights that minor-league promoters had long employed. Slurpee Night drew ten thousand people in a season where any five-figure attendance number was a cause for celebration. Hot Pants Night drew another big crowd. Then Short found himself with something fans liked more than Slurpees and hot pants.

By virtue of finishing last the year before, the Rangers got the first pick in the 1973 draft, and they signed a genuine high school phenom from just down the road at Houston Westchester High School, David Clyde, and they unveiled him to the world without him enjoying so much as a Pepsi at the minor-league level.

Clyde rewrote the Texas and national high school record book in the early '70s. By the time he graduated, Clyde was listed in fourteen separate categories in the *National High School Sports Record Book*, and the gaudy numbers he put up at Westchester still have him listed among the pitching leaders in ten categories and the all-time leader in five. Just one of two high school pitchers to ever strike out more than 300 hitters in a season, Clyde's record of 842 career strikeouts still stands, as does his thirteen shutouts in 1973. He still leads in most innings pitched without allowing an earned run—115 2/3 in 1972. Nobody in Texas or anywhere else had ever seen anything like David Clyde. Less than a month after his high school graduation, the whole country—or at least that part of it called Texas—would hang on his every pitch in his major-league debut.

While no one denied that Clyde had a ton of talent, even Herzog was less than enthused about the plan. "This ain't high school," he said. "Up here, he'll find the strike zone shrinking fast, and he won't find any 130-pound kids swinging at the high one."

Clyde made his debut on June 27, 1973, against the Minnesota Twins amid much hoopla from "Short the Showman," who had hula dancers and lion cubs entertaining fans as they filed through the turnstiles to give the Rangers their first-ever sold-out home game. Thousands more were turned away at the gates. A portion of the people who paid money to see the savior's debut missed the first pitch, which was a ball. The next several pitches missed the strike zone as well, and he had two on and no outs when he struck out Bobby Darwin, which gave the crowd its first reason to cheer. The noise reached a crescendo by the end of the inning after he struck out two more batters.

Clyde walked four and gave up a two-run home run to Mike Adams in the second inning, but he got out of it, thanks largely to catcher Piggy Suarez's throwing out Steve Braun at second. Clyde worked his way through three more innings and left after five with the Rangers ahead, 4–2. Bill Gogolewski was called in to save the game,

David Clyde went directly from high school in Houston to the Major Leagues with the Rangers. *Texas Rangers.*

and he did so by allowing just one hit the rest of the way. When Clyde was good that night, he was *very* good. The fans went home happy.

Clyde turned out to be a short-term financial pleasure for Short. The Rangers drew 218,420 fans on the twelve nights that Clyde pitched at Arlington Stadium but averaged a little better than 9,000 for the whole season. The Rangers had only drawn crowds of more than 20,000 twice during their time in Arlington. Clyde finished the season with a less-than-stellar 4-8 record and an ERA of 5.03 that flagged his lack of experience.

For that season, David Clyde was the face of the franchise, and sometimes it was a happy face—like when he gave up one run in seven innings against the Red Sox, and Carl Yastrzemski said, "In my second at bat, the kid threw as hard as any pitcher I have faced in my career. The ball seemed to come out of nowhere. He struck me out, and I wasn't surprised when he did."

If Herzog thought he would be around to help Clyde develop into a consistent major-league pitcher, he was wrong. Short fired him on September 2, just as soon as Billy Martin became available by getting himself fired in Detroit. Herzog was popular with fans, players and sportswriters, but Short was not. Getting rid of Herzog, even if the manager-in-waiting was the explosive Billy Martin, was not a popular move.

At the press conference announcing Herzog's firing, Short said, "If my mother were managing the Rangers and I had the opportunity to hire Billy Martin, I'd fire my mother. I owe it to the fans to give them my best shot, and I am hoping in time that people will be able to say this was an excellent decision."

Herzog took the news with the good humor and candor he had always shown. "I thought that the emphasis here was supposed to be more on development than winning right away," he said. "I guess I was wrong about that, and when you're wrong with a 47-91 record, you are not going to get very far."

David Clyde struggled under Billy Martin's tutelage—or lack thereof. Clyde went 3-9 in his second year with the Rangers and was 0-1 the next year before going down to the minors for the first time. A two-year major-league veteran, he saw his first minor-league dressing room when he was twenty. Clyde pitched a couple of years for another franchise with low attendance, the Cleveland Indians, and somewhere along the way developed arm problems. He tried a comeback with his hometown Houston Astros in 1981 but didn't make it out of the minors. Twenty-seven days away from being eligible for his pension from Major League Baseball, David Clyde decided he'd had enough, and he walked away from the game for good.

Despite the reputation that preceded him, Billy Martin was decidedly low key during his first spring training with the Rangers. He came across in those first days as an easygoing fellow with a smile and handshake for everybody. Martin was personable, and people were drawn to him, but all too often he ended up taking a swing at them. His temper was of the hair-trigger variety and might erupt anywhere—on the field, in the dugout or in the clubhouse—but his temper was most often on display within the confines of various drinking establishments from coast to coast. He managed the Twins for a while and led them to a pennant, but he also got into a fight with one of his pitchers in an alley. He managed Detroit for a while and did pretty well, but he once asked his pitchers to throw at opposing hitters; not only that, but he also outlined his intention to the umpires during the pre-game meeting at home plate. Not long after that, Martin went to work for Bob Short and the Rangers.

Billy Martin made the firing of Herzog look like a good move—for a while.

In 1974, under Martin, the Rangers didn't quite go from worst to first, but they finished second to Oakland with an 84-76 record. In the process, they became the only team to rise above .500 after two consecutive one-hundred-loss seasons.

Martin's good fortune in 1974 came from several players who had the best or one of the best seasons they had ever had or ever would have. The stalwart of the turnaround was Ferguson Jenkins, a future member of the Hall of Fame who came to the Rangers in a trade with the Chicago Cubs. Jenkins was thirty-one and judged by the Cubs to be past his prime, but he won twenty-five games for the Rangers and posted a 2.81 ERA while striking out 225 batters and walking just 45. He was the 1974 Comeback Player of the Year and a close second in Cy Young Award voting.

Jeff Burroughs was the American League MVP, based on the fact that the Rangers' turnaround coincided with his twenty-five home runs, 118 RBIs and .301 batting average. Mike Hargrove, from Perryton, was the first native Texan to play for the Rangers. (Clyde was considered a hometown kid, but his family moved to Houston when he was a freshman in high school.) Hargrove hit .323 for the Rangers and was the A.L. Rookie of the Year. Billy Martin was named Manager of the Year, which surprised no one. Nor was it much of a shock when he was fired after the Rangers fell to earth with a thud in 1975, a year when *Baseball Digest* and other publications had picked Texas to win the pennant.

Short didn't fire Martin. Brad Corbett, head of an investor group that bought the team one week into the 1974 season, would have that pleasure. He also had the pleasure of seeing fans go out to the park as the team drew more than one million spectators for the first time. And if Corbett did take pleasure in hiring and firing managers, he must have been very happy indeed with the Rangers. He hired Frank Lucchesi to take over for Martin. Lucchesi stayed at the helm until 1977, at which point Eddie Stanky was hired as manager for a couple days, followed by a short stint from Connie Ryan and finally Billy Hunter. The Rangers were 60-33 the rest of the way under Hunter. They put together an impressive 94-68 record but finished eight games out of first place.

Much as 1974 had been, 1977 was a turnaround year for the Rangers. Bert Blyleven threw the Rangers' second no-hitter. Doyle Alexander led the pitching staff in wins, with seventeen, followed by thirty-six-year-old Gaylord Perry, with a 15-12 record in the twilight of his career. Dock Ellis, perhaps best known for pitching a perfect game for the Pirates while high on LSD, went 10-6 with a 2.90 ERA. But in time, and not very much of it, Hunter was replaced by Pat Corrales, a Rangers coach since '75.

Despite strong performances from Al Oliver (.324 average), catcher Jim Sundberg (dependable behind the plate and with a .278 average) and Bobby Bonds (thirty-one home runs), in 1978 the Rangers' record dropped to 87-75, five games out of first place. An 83-79 record the following year brought them to the same point, but in 1980, the Rangers tumbled to 76-85, twenty games behind the leaders. Harrah was gone, traded to the Indians for all-star third baseman Buddy Bell, who would become a fixture in the Rangers' lineup for many years and a fan favorite.

Other Corbett deals did not work out so well, such as a trade that sent Dave Righetti to the Yankees for Sparky Lyle. Hargrove was traded along with Bobby Bonds, Len Hargrove and several others. Corbett and the Rangers' front office labored under the illusion that they were just one player away from winning a pennant. Despite a flurry of trades and managerial changes, Corbett never found that one player. Or manager.

In 1981, the strike-shortened season, the Rangers came as close to a pennant as they would for a long time. On June 11, 1981, Fergie Jenkins and the Rangers blew a 3–1 sixth-inning lead against the Milwaukee Brewers and ended up losing, 6–3, one day before the strike began. Had Texas held on to win that game, it would have clinched a playoff spot, but it didn't, and it would be a long time before the Rangers would contend again.

THE PSYCHEDELIC '70S

The Houston Astros of the 1970s were a colorful team but not always a good one. The team was noted for its colorful uniforms as much and sometimes more than its play on the field. The first change came in 1971 when the Astro uniforms emphasized the orange at the expense of the navy blue, which now came in a slightly paler shade.

In 1975, the uniforms transformed into an explosion of color that Peter Max must have appreciated but a lot of old-time baseball fans, players and sportswriters did not. Other teams had added color to their uniforms before the Astros went what a lot of people considered overboard. When the Atlanta Braves added color to their jerseys and some tiled art flowers to their sleeves, Houston's Doug Rader heckled them in warm-ups: "What'll it be tonight, boys? Slow-pitch or fast-pitch?"

Unbeknownst to Rader, his own team had hired an advertising firm to "rebrand" the Astros, and its creation, unveiled to the world in April 1975, opened to the kind of reviews that would have closed an art show. A common complaint was that the new uniforms made the players look like popsicles, and it was hard to take them seriously. Others compared the uniforms to rainbows and nightmares. Mostly, they were called the rainbow jerseys and featured broad stripes of orange, yellow, red and even a little pink splashed across the front. More often than not, people said the uniforms made the Astros look like a softball team. Rader, mercifully in this regard, was traded to the San Diego Padres.

Other than the uniforms, Astro bright spots were hard to find on the field in the early '70s. Larry Dierker pitched well enough to be named to the 1971 National League all-star team. In September of that year, J.R. Richard made his major-league debut against the San Francisco Giants and struck out fifteen, the most in any major-league debut since 1954.

By 1972, the Astros had perked up, thanks in part to a lineup that was suddenly more Punch and less Judy. Lee May, part of the Joe Morgan trade, led the team with twenty-nine home runs. Jim Wynn hit twenty-four, and the irascible Rader (a main character in Jim Bouton's controversial bestseller *Ball Four*) and Cesar Cedeno each hit twenty-two. Dierker and Wilson anchored an otherwise unimpressive pitching staff with fifteen wins apiece.

While the Astros hardly set the league on fire, they did finish with the best record in their history, 84-69, in the strike-shortened '72 season. Houston responded to this initial flush of success by firing manager Harry "the Hat" Walker and replacing him with Leo Durocher. The Astros responded the next year with a disappointing 82-80 record. The pitching, not that strong to begin with, deteriorated further as Dierker missed much of the year with an arm injury, and Wilson struggled. In January 1975, Wilson and his five-year-old son died from carbon monoxide poisoning. The team honored Wilson by retiring his number, forty, in April of that year, the same year the Astros unveiled their rainbow uniforms to the world.

Meanwhile, the "Eighth Wonder of the World," the Astrodome, was slipping from Hofheinz's grip. The judge, with the Astrodomian $38 million in debt, was going Astro-broke. Not in the best of health, Hofheinz had neither the desire nor the ability to rebuild the crumbling empire. Eventually, Hofheinz lost control of the Astros and the Astrodome to GE Credit and Ford Motor Credit. The corporate owners/creditors drove the team like a mid-sized sedan in an era of Cadillacs. Tal Smith returned to Houston from the New York Yankees as general manager and was tasked with rebuilding the team but without a lot of money with which to work.

Ownership's frugality and apathy would hamstring the team for years. The players wearing the psychedelic uniforms and the managers who managed them did their best to keep the team respectable, but it didn't always work out that way. The 1975 Astros finished at 64-97, worse even than their debut years as the Colt .45s.

Under new manager Bill Virdon, the 1976 Astros surged to 80-82. Jose Cruz, acquired from the St. Louis Cardinals for a mere $25,000, took over in left field and would play with the Astros for twelve years and later served the team as a first base coach.

Art Howe, a journeyman infielder anxious to catch on with any team, became a valuable player for the Astros primarily at third base, but he was versatile enough to play shortstop and second. Richard, Joe Niekro—another player seemingly on his way out of baseball before catching on with Houston—and Andujar anchored a pitching staff that otherwise remained thin around the edges.

The Astros of that era added more stability to the lineup by trading with Seattle for shortstop Craig Reynolds and catcher Alan Ashby, two more players who played key roles for the Astros for several seasons to come. After a 74-88 record in 1978, the Astros came out

Art Howe was a key member of the Astros and later managed the team.

of the gate the next year with a no-hitter by Ken Forsch against the Braves in the second game of the year. A month later, Dr. John McMullen agreed to buy the Astros, giving the team something it badly needed: a real owner.

It might have looked like McMullen was sinking his money into a losing proposition—a team that even some fans derided as the "Las-tros"—but the '79 team made McMullen look positively psychic. The team was built to fit the spacious confines of the Astrodome with an emphasis on pitching, defense and speed. While Tris Speaker's glove might have been the place where triples went to die, the three-bagger lived at the Astrodome in '79; the Astros had fifty-two triples, including nine by Reynolds, but only forty-two home runs in a year that saw the total number of home runs increase by 18 percent. Cruz led the Astros in home runs, with nine.

This was also the era of Bob Watson, who got even less recognition than the badly underrated Cruz but was a model of consistency at the plate and at first base. Drafted as a catcher in 1965, he took over at first base for Houston after Joe Pepitone left the team to deal with some legal problems back in New York. The legal matters took longer than Pepitone expected, and by the time he came back, Watson was the Astros' regular first baseman. He hit .300 or better four times for Houston and twice drove in more than one hundred runs. He hit for the cycle—a single, double, triple and home run in the same game—for Houston in 1977 and pulled off the same feat for the Boston Red Sox in 1979.

Joe Niekro, who learned the knuckleball from his brother Phil, used that pitch to reestablish his career with Houston, going from so-so journeyman to a twenty-one-game winner with the Astros in 1979. While he did not use the knuckleball exclusively, he used it to great effect in combination with his fastball and slider and would become the first Astro pitcher to win twenty or more games in consecutive seasons when he won twenty the following year.

Richard had developed into one of the most overpowering pitchers in the league, winning eighteen games in '79 and striking out 313 in 292 innings, and Joe Sambito was lights out from the bullpen. Despite the lack of gaudy offensive numbers, the pitching was good enough to propel the Astros to a ten-game lead by July, but Cincinnati pulled ahead in the final month of the season, finishing a game and a half in front of the colorful but no longer derided Astros, who could point to an 89-73 record—their best yet—as a promising starting point.

The excitement reached something just short of shrieking hysteria when McMullen showed he was willing to negotiate with the Big Boys for free agents by agreeing to Major League Baseball's first million-dollar player contract. Not only that, but the signee and first million-dollar player was a local boy who had gone first to New York and later to California to become something of a legend. Nolan Ryan was coming home, and he was bringing his fastball with him.

Ryan was thirty-two years old and fresh from a storied eight years with the California Angels, where he threw four no-hitters, tying Sandy Koufax's major-league record, and made the Mets look as bad for trading him as the Astros looked after they traded Joe Morgan. In his first year with the Angels in 1972, Ryan struck out 329 batters and allowed the fewest hits per inning of anybody in major-league history. That might have been considered a career year, but Ryan would go on to better his strikeout total in four of the next five years. He struck out 383 batters in 1973, eclipsing Koufax's major-league record by 1. He threw two no-hitters that year, including one against Detroit in which he struck out 17, and threw no-hitters in each of the next two years. He also had seven one-hitters, which tied him with Koufax for the most ever.

The Angels rarely contended for a pennant during Ryan's eight years in Anaheim, and his win-loss record was average, but nearly every other number he put fell into the eye-popping category. The Angels finally made the playoffs in 1979, Ryan's last year in California, and Ryan pitched seven innings in game one of the National League Championship Series (NLCS) against Baltimore ace Jim Palmer, but neither pitcher figured in the decision.

Ryan entered the free agent market, and he drew a lot of takers, including George Steinbrenner of the New York Yankees, whom it was rumored would pay as much as—gasp!—$1 million dollars to sign the man known as the Ryan Express. Houston, Texas and Milwaukee were also in the mix, but Ryan wanted very badly to pitch in Houston, just half an hour from his home in Alvin, and McMullen agreed to agree with Ryan on professional sports' first million-dollar player contract. He teamed with Richard, Niekro and Forsch to form one of the most fearsome rotations in baseball.

Richard, after years of brilliance with intermittent bouts of extreme wildness, had developed into one of the game's most feared pitchers. He began the season with five straight wins and an ERA under 2.00; at one point, he threw three straight complete-game shutouts. On July 3, in a 5–3 win over the Braves, he broke Dierker's team record of 1,487 strikeouts.

And yet, J.R. Richard was not fully embraced by the Astros, their fans or the sportswriters who covered the team. He complained of a "dead arm" and of neck, back and shoulder

J.R. Richard seemed destined for the Hall of Fame until he was felled by a stroke.

problems. The general consensus in the media was that Richard was a malcontent and a whiner, and he received buckets of bad ink even as he was putting together as good a season as any pitcher in baseball. "He had the greatest stuff I've seen," Joe Morgan once said. "It gives me goose bumps to think of what he might have become." Morgan, as a free agent, had rejoined the Astros in hopes of helping them to their first playoffs and World Series.

On July 30, 1980, Richard collapsed while going through pre-game warm-ups with the team. He was rushed to Southern Methodist Hospital, where only emergency surgery saved his life. His career, however, was over. The remorse and regret came spilling out from fans and sportswriters almost as soon as Richard hit the ground, but they didn't get the chance to make it up to him because he was through, well short of what everybody assumed would be a stop in the Baseball Hall of Fame at Cooperstown.

Without Richard, the team began to struggle. What had looked like a sure trip to Houston's first postseason series began to look like another year of "would, coulda, shoulda" as the Astros tumbled from atop the division to third place before regaining the lead with a ten-game winning streak. They went to Los Angeles for the final three games of the season, leading the National League West by three games, and lost all three games.

The scene at the Astrodome after the Astros finally clinched a playoff berth. *Houston Astros.*

That necessitated a one-game playoff with the Dodgers for the right to face the Phillies in the divisional series. Niekro pitched in that game and allowed just one unearned run in going the distance. After Houston scored a couple of unearned runs in the first, Howe hit a two-run home run in the third for a 4–0 Houston lead and drove in two more runs with a bases-loaded single in the fourth as Houston went on to win, 7–1. There was little time to celebrate; the first game of the National League Division Series (NLDS) was scheduled the next day in Philadelphia.

The Phillies started Steve Carlton, who had beat the Astros six times that season, in game one, made it seven with a 3–1 win, the Phillies' first home playoff win since 1915. The Astros got the first ever playoff win the next day as Ryan started on the mound and gave up two runs over six-plus innings in a 7–4 Astros victory.

Back home in the dome for game three, the first major-league playoff game to be played indoors, Houston put Niekro on the mound, and he was superb, working his way out of jam after jam, helped in no small part by two nice plays from Cruz in left field that helped keep the game scoreless. Morgan tripled to lead off the eleventh and was replaced by Rafael Landestoy as a pinch runner. Denny Walling's sacrifice fly scored him with the game-winner. Manager Bill Virdon's decision to pinch run for Morgan led to a rift between the two that in turn led to Morgan leaving Houston the next season, this time for good.

Game four has been described as one of the most grueling and exciting playoff games in major-league history and featured five double plays, including four that were started by outfielders and a triple play that wasn't.

That happened in the fourth inning with two Phillies on base. Maddox hit a soft liner to pitcher Vern Ruhle, who snagged the ball and threw to Art Howe at first. The home plate umpire ruled that Ruhle had trapped the ball, but the first and third base umpires said that Ruhle had caught the ball on the fly. Howe, taking no chances, raced to second base for what he thought was a triple play. The Phillies disagreed loudly and vehemently. Twenty minutes later, following a twenty-minute umpire conference that came to include American League President Chub Feeney, it was decided that since time had been called before Howe ran to second, the third out didn't count. Close, but no triple play. The Phillies went on to win, 5–3, in extra innings.

"This was a strange game where strange things happened," Virdon commented. "Not a lot of things were new today; I just never saw so many of them in one game."

In the deciding game five, the Astros went with the veteran Ryan while Philadelphia manager Dallas Green went with rookie Marty Bystrom. Ryan, in control through most of the game, ran into trouble in the eighth when the Phillies loaded the bases with nobody out. Pete Rose, who would go on to have the most hits in the history of the game, faced Ryan, who would go on to have more strikeouts than anybody in history. Rose walked. Relief ace Joe Sambito was called in to put out the fire against pinch-hitter Keith Moreland, a former football and baseball star at UT. Moreland grounded weakly to Morgan at second, but a run scored, trimming the Astros' lead to 5–4. Al Unser tied the game with a single, and Manny Trillo tripled to put the Phillies up 7–5.

Houston, true to form, battled back to tie the game in the bottom of the eighth on two-out RBI singles by Landestoy and Cruz, but Philadelphia won it in the eleventh.

"That's about as even a series as you'll ever find," Sambito said after the game. "Some guys might take it harder than others, but I'm proud to be an Astro."

The players' strike that probably killed the Texas Rangers' playoff chances in 1981 played out in the Astros' favor. They finished third in the overall National League West standings, but the strike resulted in the cancellation of fifty-two games.

Major League Baseball decided to split the season into two halves and have the division winner of each "half" play each other for the division crown. Under that format, Houston and Los Angeles met in a best-of-five format. The Cincinnati Reds, who had a better overall record than either team, missed out on postseason play because they didn't win either "half." Houston actually had the third-best record in the division (61-49), but it had to like its chances against the Dodgers because the Astros had Nolan Ryan and the Dodgers had shown that they had a hard time hitting Ryan.

On September 26, the thirty-four-year-old veteran, whom many assumed was in the twilight of his career, broke the tie with Sandy Koufax for the most no-hitters in major-league history when he threw the fifth no-hitter of his career. It came in the midst of a pennant race, which Houston was suddenly in the thick of with the new format. The game was broadcast nationally on NBC, making it one of the most viewed no-hitters in history. The Dodgers were the victims of Nolan's Ryan's historic game, which came six years after his fourth no-hitter. Ryan said he didn't feel like he had his best stuff, especially in the late innings, but credited his curve ball, not his fastball, for the win.

Nolan Ryan was a threat to throw a no-hitter every time he took the mound.

"The key was my curve ball," Ryan said after the game. "You can't win with one pitch. It doesn't matter how fast you can throw, but with a curve they had to think about the breaking ball."

Ryan struggled with his control early with a couple of walks and a wild pitch, but he had his strikeout pitch going, and this was the 135th time Ryan had struck out at least ten batters in a game. A brilliant running catch by Terry Puhl in right field was the defensive gem of the day. At season's end, Ryan led the league with a miniscule 1.69 ERA.

In the opening game of the playoff series, the Dodgers again had to face Ryan. They had better luck against him this time around; they managed two hits. A two-run home run by Ashby in the bottom of the ninth won it for the Astros. In game two, Niekro didn't have his best stuff but always seemed to make the pitch he had to make when he had to make it to keep Los Angeles off the scoreboard. Dave Smith and Sambito relieved in tenth and eleventh innings, respectively, and the Astros finally won it on a bases-loaded, pinch-hit single by Denny Walling in the bottom of the eleventh. Up to this point, the Dodgers had failed to score a single run against Houston pitching in twenty innings.

Houston traveled to Los Angeles needing just one win to advance to the league championship. Burt Hooton, a former University of Texas standout, three-hit the Astros in game three, a 6–1 Los Angeles victory. Left-handed sensation Fernando Valenzuela tossed a four-hitter that was good enough for a 2–1 victory in game four, despite a performance from Houston's Vern Ruhle that was almost the match of Valenzuela's gem.

Los Angeles closed out Houston's hopes in game five, getting to Ryan for three runs in the sixth as part of a 4–0 win. Jerry Reuss got the win for the Dodgers. The Astros were out of the playoffs but not out of the discussion of up-and-coming National League teams. For the first time, people didn't laugh when the terms "National League pennant" and "Houston Astros" were mentioned in the same breath.

Turn for the Better

While professional sports suffered in the 1980s from a wide range of ills, including drug scandals, player strikes and rapidly escalating salaries, the Texas League shook off the doldrums of the 1970s and marched past the million mark in attendance. Fans had figured out that they could see the stars of tomorrow today at a fraction of the cost of a major-league game.

The Texas League turnaround was perhaps most apparent in El Paso, where Jim Paul took a struggling franchise and turned it into one of the Texas League's premier attractions by making the game itself a mere starting point for a party. Baseball had a long history in El Paso, going back to 1884, when the town team El Paso Browns edged out a team from Fort Bliss, 18–17. John McCloskey, founder of the Texas League, also founded the Class D Rio Grande League in 1915, which featured an El Paso team. El Paso in legend and lore was always a favorite hangout and way station for outlaws, and El Paso participated for a while in the outlaw Copper League, notorious for the fact that players banned from or shunned by the big leagues, like Hal Chase, played in it.

El Paso fielded teams for various minor leagues for many years before breaking through as a Class AA team in the Texas League in 1962. The Sun Kings drew 148,000 fans their first year in the league and won the pennant going away behind future major leaguers like Jesus Alou and Felix Maldonado. But by 1970, the team's fortunes were sagging. In 1973, the Sun Kings drew just 63,081 fans.

Jim Paul was a sports information director at Southwestern Louisiana University when he was offered a job as the general manager of the El Paso Sun Kings. By his own admission, he didn't know a lot about baseball, but he had a flair for promotion, and the ownership group that owned the team was open to ideas. Among the first changes Paul made was changing the name of the team to the Diablos, Spanish for "devil." Then he had the stands painted bright yellow. He brought in Brooklyn-born Paul Strelzin as the public address announcer and turned him loose as a cheerleader for the Diablos and a heckler of opposing teams. When an opposing manager complained to league president Bobby Bragan about Strelzin, Bragan pointed to the Diablos' attendance figures and suggested his team might want to try something similar.

In El Paso, the ball game turned out to be merely the starting point for a party. Upon entering Dudley Field, Diablo fans were handed tissues. They knew to wave them whenever an opposing pitcher left the game as the PA blared Janis Joplin's "Bye Bye Baby." Under Paul's guidance and his gleeful approval, the team built what was billed as the world's largest banana split and issued spoons to the youngest fans so they could eat it. There were fireworks and giveaways, promotions and entertainment. Something special was going on nearly every night at the ballpark. Attendance soared, going from a paltry 63,081 in 1973, the year before Paul was hired, to more than 200,000 in 1977. The former small-college sports information director was named the *Sporting News* Minor League Executive of the Year for two straight years. Heckled in turn by others in baseball for some of his promotions and gimmicks, his success in El Paso led others to try the same thing, as Bragan had suggested. By and large, it worked.

The rest of the Texas League, through a shifting set of franchises that came to include teams from beyond the state's borders, also enjoyed a resurgence. The league had drawn ten million fans in 1963 and had doubled that number by the end of the 1970s. The level of play was outstanding, and sometimes better than that. On July 16, 1978, some two hundred fans saw one of the best pitching performances of that or any other year when Dave Righetti, pitching for the Tulsa Drillers against the Midland Cubs, struck out eighteen batters over nine innings. He struck out the side in the second and third innings and at one point struck out seven in a row. He left the game with the record for most strikeouts in a nine-inning game, breaking the record set in 1909 by Willie Mitchell of San Antonio against the Galveston Sand Crabs, but he felt like he'd failed after giving up the tying run in the ninth inning. He left with the game tied at two apiece, and Tulsa went on to lose, 4–2, in extra innings.

Righetti, the number one pick of the Texas Rangers, had fallen a bit out of favor with the Rangers after some shaky starts, but Rangers' pitching instructor Dick Such said it was the best pitching performance he had ever seen. A scout for the New York Yankees was also at the game and probably wasn't as bothered by the fact that Righetti went on the disabled list with tendinitis in his bicep as were the Rangers, who were inclined to write him off as sore-armed. In negotiations with the Yankees for pitcher Sparky Lyle, the Rangers threw in Righetti as more or less a bonus piece in a ten-player deal. Righetti went on to win the American League Rookie of the Year Award with the Yankees in 1981, the same year that David Clyde was knocking around the Astros' minor-league system in a final and futile comeback attempt.

Tom Grieve was with the Rangers as a scout and assistant to farm director Joe Klein in 1981, a couple years after he hung up his spikes for good. Growing up in Massachusetts, where the winters are long and the high school baseball seasons are short, Grieve didn't have as much time to impress scouts as did the players from warmer climes, but he impressed the Washington Senators enough that they chose him as their number one pick in 1966.

Despite being a first-round pick, Grieve made his way to the Major Leagues the hard way, by working his way through the various rungs of the Senators' minor-league system, making his first appearance with the Senators in 1970. His first full season in the Major Leagues was in 1972, the first year the franchise was in Texas. As a player, Grieve was solid without being spectacular. He played mostly as a reserve or platoon player and hit anywhere from .204 to .309. In six years with the Rangers, he played for six different managers, not counting two others who served on an interim basis, though it might be true that the job itself was an interim position.

In 1977, Corbett traded Grieve to the New York Mets. He played there for a year that was mostly forgettable but fortuitous in one respect: he met and became good friends with Bobby Valentine, who impressed Grieve not only with his insights into the game but also with his drive to excel and win. Grieve was traded to St. Louis the next year and released; he ended the 1979 season as an outfielder with the Rangers' Triple A affiliate in the Pacific Coast League, Tucson. Clearly, he decided, it was time for a change.

When Corbett offered him a front office job in ticket sales and promotions, Grieve took it and worked a series of front office jobs, becoming a scout and assistant to farm director Joe Klein. Grieve took over as farm director when Klein was promoted to general manager, and when Klein "resigned"

TOM
GRIEVE
TEXAS RANGERS   **OUTFIELD**

Tom Grieve was with the Washington Senators and made the transition to Texas with the Rangers.

in 1984, Rangers' president Mike Stone offered the job to the thirty-six-year-old Grieve.

Grieve took the Rangers' general manager job at a time when the team and the franchise seemed to be in freefall. Corbett had sold the team to Eddie

Chiles in 1980, when Chiles was seventy years old and angry. Chiles's story was one of rags to riches, from living hand-to-mouth to owning the Western Company of North America, a Fortune 500 company. He was famous in the '70s for an ongoing series of self-financed radio ads in which he declared, "I'm Eddie Chiles, and I'm mad as hell!" Bumper stickers appeared that read: "I'm mad, too, Eddie!"

Chiles's version of free enterprise maintained a dim view of such baseball market anomalies as free agency, which he generally avoided by signing less talented players for less money. The financial realities of owning a Major League Baseball team in the '80s took Chiles by surprise.

"Yeah, I've asked myself what the hell am I doing here," he said in a 1982 press conference. "I guess I'm about like the mouse who said I'm not after the cheese anymore. I'm just trying to get my head out of the trap."

Chiles would try to rid himself of the Rangers several times, especially as his Western Company's fortunes also began to slide. He tried to sell out to Gaylord Broadcasting, but American League owners didn't want another broadcasting company turning a team in a superstation entry. A New York syndicate was interested but wouldn't promise to keep the team in Texas.

When Chiles's Western Company went bankrupt, he became less choosy about where the team ended up and announced that he intended to sell the team to an investment group that would move the franchise to Tampa. Commissioner Peter Ueberroth brokered a sale to a consortium headed by George W. Bush, whose father was serving as president of the United States at the time. Chiles was mad as hell and threatened to take the whole matter to court because he didn't like Ueberroth running his business, but in the end he sold to the Bush group.

Doug Rader was a solid player with Houston but had his problems as manager of the Rangers.

115

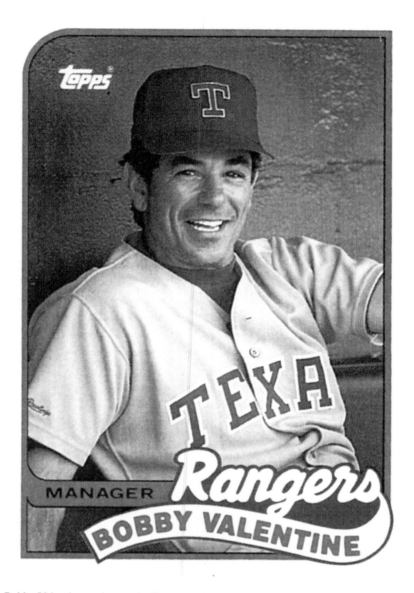

Bobby Valentine took over the Rangers after Rader was fired.

On the field, the Rangers were manager Doug Rader's problem. Rader was already one of baseball's legendary characters, a reputation helped along by Bouton's portrayal of him in *Ball Four*. Rader was the original "wild and crazy guy" who urged Little Leaguers to eat baseball cards, the better to digest all the information they contained.

As a manager of the Rangers, Rader was still a wild and crazy guy, but his confrontations with players, fans and sportswriters sometimes bordered on the felonious. The Rangers were up and down early in Rader's first season in 1983, but the team got hot in June and moved into first place. A day before the all-star game, they broke a 4–4 tie in the fifteenth inning by sending sixteen batters to the plate and scoring twelve runs. But the team slumped badly after the break and finished fourth, under .500. The slump was punctuated by Rader's occasional and then fairly frequent fits of rage. Rader coached the team for two more years and committed one public relations blunder after another, hampered further by Chiles's parsimonious restrictions. Finally, Rader was fired early in the 1985 season and replaced by Grieve's old buddy from the Mets, Bobby Valentine.

Valentine had told Grieve he wanted to manage someday, and Grieve believed that Valentine had what it takes to be a good manager. The kicker was that Valentine had never served as a manager of even one baseball game, and he had a good job as third base coach of a New York Mets team that had every reasonable expectation of going to a World Series soon. Grieve goaded Valentine into taking the job, telling him, "Anybody can stay with the Mets. Coaching third base for the Mets is a good situation. It would take a special man to take on the job we are offering—to turn around the Texas Rangers."

In the end, Valentine took the job because he knew that Grieve was right—he would probably never be offered a job as challenging as the one his old friend was pitching. He also knew that he might never get the chance to work for Grieve again.

"The Rangers and Senators have trashed 13 managers in fifteen seasons," Randy Galloway wrote for the *Dallas Morning News*. "Manager Bobby Valentine obviously needs your prayers. Tom Grieve, the third general manager in four years, needs your prayers. Pray for the entire franchise. Pray for rain."

The Astros, denizens of the Astrodome, didn't have the luxury of praying for rain. The playoff appearance in 1981 did not, as it turned out, foreshadow a playoff run in 1982. Manager Bill Virdon was fired late in the season, and Bob Lillis, an original member of the Colt .45s, was hired to take his place.

Other changes were soon forthcoming. Pitcher Don Sutton was traded to the Milwaukee Brewers for three prospects that included Kevin Bass, who would become a mainstay. Ditto second baseman Bill Doran, who was called up from the minors late in the year and didn't leave. Pitcher Mike Scott was acquired from the Mets for outfielder Danny Heep, a move that lowered the median age of the pitching staff by several years.

Scott didn't pay immediate dividends. He won ten games in 1983, his first full season with Houston, but slipped badly to a 5-11 mark in 1984. The Astros deserve some credit for sticking with Scott, who looked for all the world like another pitcher with a great future behind him. He had come to the team with a 14-27 record with the Mets and showed no signs of turning the corner until pitching coach Roger Craig worked with him a bit and

Mike Scott was one of the best pitchers in Houston history and threw one of the timeliest no-hitters in history. *Houston Astros.*

showed him a "new" pitch: the split-fingered fastball. The pitch is hard to throw and a bit risky; if it hangs instead of dropping, it is begging to be knocked out of the park. In the hands of someone who knows how to use the pitch, it can be devastating to hitters as they take a swing at the ball at the same time as it drops several inches out of the strike zone. Scott went on to win eighty-six games over the next five years and in 1986 became Houston's first Cy Young Award winner as the best pitcher in the National League.

As Scott was rounding into his own, Nolan Ryan continued to defy time and baffle opposing hitters. In 1983, at age thirty-six, he surpassed Walter Johnson's all-time strikeout record of 3,508. The next season, he became the first pitcher to reach 4,000 strikeouts when he fanned Danny Heep on July 11.

Craig Reynolds became the starting shortstop when Dickie Thon was hit in the face by a pitch and had to miss nearly all of the 1984 season. Glenn Davis came up from the minors because nobody down there could get him out, or even keep him in the ballpark, and he immediately provided some much-needed power to the Astros' lineup. Niekro, the Astros' leading pitcher in wins to that point, with 144, was traded at the end of the 1985 season. Billy Hatcher came over from the Cubs and found a home in the dome.

Prior to the 1986 season, general manager Al Rosen and Lillis were fired to make room for Dick Wagner in the front office and Hal Lanier in the dugout. Lanier, a disciple of Whitey Herzog, promoted a style of ball perfectly fitted to the Astrodome and the Houston lineup. "Whiteyball" emphasized speed, pitching and defense and put less of a premium on home runs. It paid big dividends in 1986, Houston's silver anniversary season.

The Astros broke out of the gate quickly with Scott, Ryan and Bob Knepper starting and winning most of the games and a bullpen anchored by closer Dave Smith and long relief man Charley Kerfeld holding down the fort in the late innings. Catcher Alan Ashby emerged as a solid, injury-free starting catcher with the pleasurable chore of handling one of the best staffs in baseball.

Rookie Jim Deshaies worked his way into the starting rotation to bolster the pitching staff even more, but the Astros slipped to second place by the all-star break. Accustomed to late-season swoons, fans were slow to jump on the bandwagon, but this year's team was different. Not only did this team hold on during a gritty pennant race, but the Astros also responded to the season's most critical moments with dramatic performances.

On September 23, Deshaies struck out the first eight Dodgers he faced, setting a modern major-league record in the process, as part of a two-hit shutout. The next night, Ryan pitched six innings of no-hit ball before surrendering a single in the seventh. He struck out the side in the eighth, giving him twelve for the night. Kerfeld closed it out in the ninth. The win put Houston in a mathematical tie for first place going into the final game of the home stand against the Giants. Lanier sent Scott to the mound with hopes that Houston could clinch the division title at home in front of fans who were actually starting to believe that theirs was a team that might win a division and even a World Series.

Scott didn't let them down. In front of 32,808 fans, he threw a no-hitter to clinch the title, the first division- or pennant-clinching no-hitter in modern major-league history since Allie Reynolds of the Yankees kept the Red Sox hitless in the first game of a double-header to clinch a tie for the American League pennant in 1951. It was the first Astros no-hitter since Nolan Ryan's fifth in 1981.

Scott said later this his split-fingered pitch was working as well as it ever had, and the Giants had no reason to doubt it. Scott struck out 13 and at one point retired 14 straight in the Astros' historic 2–0 win. The win also probably clinched the National League Cy Young Award for Scott, the first ever won by a Houston pitcher. Aside from his eighteen victories, Scott also led the league in ERA at 2.22 and strikeouts with 306.

The win put Houston in the NLDS to face the Mets, who, like the Astros, were celebrating a silver anniversary. The two sad-sack expansion teams of 1962 were now, a quarter of a century later, going to play for the right to play in the World Series. The smart money was on the Mets, winners of 108 games with one of the most formidable lineups in baseball that included Darryl Strawberry, Lenny Dykstra and Gary Carter. The Mets' pitching staff was anchored by 1985 Cy Young Award–winner Dwight Gooden, who got the call to start game one of the NLCS against Houston. The Astros countered with Scott. Scott won, 1–0, on a home run by Davis.

The Mets got to Ryan for five runs in game two, and Ron Darling, a former Ranger prospect that got away, held Houston to a single run. In New York for game three, Houston was up 5–4 in the ninth when Dykstra delivered a game-winning two-run home run off Smith.

Deshaies was scheduled to pitch game four, but when it was postponed a day because of rain, Lanier decided to go with Scott again. Good move. Scott so thoroughly baffled the Mets that they accused him of "scuffing" the baseball. They collected a bag of balls that they said showed signs of surreptitious scuffing, but league officials declared that the balls looked just fine to them.

Another kind of controversy marked game five in a match-up of Ryan and Gooden. The controversy came in the second inning when first base umpire Fred Brocklander blew a call at first base by calling Reynolds out on an inning-ending double play. The Astros argued the call long and hard, but the call stood. Replays showed that Reynolds beat the throw by a good margin. The double play prevented a runner from scoring from third, and the Astros went on to lose, 2–1, in twelve innings.

That gave the Mets a 3–2 advantage in the series going into game six. The Mets looked at it as a "must-win" game because a game seven meant they would have to face Scott again, and they didn't want that. The game that resulted is considered one of the best playoff games ever. It had great pitching, clutch hitting, another blown call by Brocklander and comebacks galore in a sixteen-inning thriller. It was a game that left both teams and their fans exhausted and emotionally spent after more than four hours of heart-stopping drama. It was the longest postseason game in major-league history.

It didn't start out that way. The Astros roughed up Mets' starter Bob Ojeda for three runs in the first. That looked to be more than enough for Knepper, who handcuffed the Mets on two hits through the first eight innings. Unfortunately for the Astros, things got interesting in the top of the ninth.

Lenny Dykstra led off with a triple and scored on a single by Mookie Wilson. When Hernandez followed with a double to drive home Wilson and close the gap to 3–2, Lanier pulled Knepper and brought in Smith, among the league leaders with a club-record thirty-three saves, to seal the deal. He promptly walked Carter and Strawberry to load the bases. Smith appeared to strike out Knight, but Brocklander, stationed behind the plate for game six, called it a ball. Knight lifted a sacrifice fly on the next pitch to tie the game at 3–3. Smith fanned Heep to send the game into extra innings—a lot of extra innings.

Mets reliever Roger McDowell shut the Astros down through the next five innings, and Smith and Larry Andersen did the same for Houston until Wally Backman singled home a run in the top of the fourteenth inning. With one out in the bottom of the inning, Billy Hatcher hit one of the most famous home runs in Houston history, a rocket shot high off the foul pole in left to tie the game at 4–4.

The Mets pulled ahead in the top of the sixteenth when Strawberry doubled off Aurelio Lopez and Knight drove him home for a 5–4 lead. When they scored twice more in the inning for what looked to be a

Roger Clemens was a star at the University of Texas who pitched in Houston long enough to fuel a couple of playoff runs. *Houston Astros.*

commanding 7–4 lead, some Houston fans began to head for the exits. In the bottom of the inning, with one out, veteran Davey Lopes pinch-hit and drew a walk, followed by hits from Doran and Hatcher to make it a 7–5 game. Davis singled home another run to pull Houston to within one, but Orosco struck out Bass to end the game and Houston's World Series hopes.

Lanier managed to be philosophical about coming out on the losing end of what people were already calling the greatest game ever. "If we had to lose a ball game, I'm glad it happened the way it did," he said. "And that was to see us going down battling the way we had the whole year."

Dykstra, with his team set to face the Boston Red Sox in the World Series, said he doubted the series could match the NLCS for drama, but he was wrong. That series, considered to be one of the best ever, is remembered for high and low drama, including Bill Buckner's error that gave the Mets new life and allowed them to go on to win the series.

Boston had some fans in Texas for that series, and not only because it was hard to pull for the Mets after such a crushing loss. The Red Sox's designated hitter, Don Baylor, grew up in Austin and played for Stephen F. Austin High School.

Three other Red Sox—pitchers Roger Clemens and Calvin Schiraldi and shortstop Spike Owen—all played for the University of Texas under coach Gustafson.

Clemens is perhaps the best-known UT baseball alum, but Gustafson didn't recruit him out of Spring Woods High School in Houston. The big-league scouts came around, but Clemens, sensing he wasn't ready, signed with San Jacinto Junior College and pitched there for two years before

Gustafson recruited him to Texas, where Clemens went 25-7 over two seasons. Gustafson has said that Burt Hooton was the best pitcher he had at UT but that Clemens was the best pro prospect. The Red Sox drafted Clemens in 1983, and he was on the mound in Fenway Park a year later. Two years after that, he won twenty-four games for the Red Sox and captured the first of what would be seven Cy Young Awards, the most ever. On April 29, 1986, he became the first major-league pitcher in history to strike out twenty batters in a nine-inning game, a feat he would later duplicate against the Detroit Tigers.

After twelve seasons and 192 wins in Boston, Clemens signed with the Toronto Blue Jays and later with the New York Yankees before coming home to play with the Houston Astros, along with fellow Texan Andy Pettite, from 2004 to 2006 and finishing his career with the New York Yankees in 2007.

In Arlington, the Texas Rangers had reason to be excited, too. After a gloomy 62-99 record in Bobby Valentine's first full year as manager, the Rangers won eighty-seven games in 1986 and finished in second place. Popular and productive third baseman Buddy Bell was traded away, and the Rangers, with exceptions like thirty-six-year-old knuckleballer Charlie Hough, began to build a team around young players like Bobby Witt and Pete Incaviglia, who hit an NCAA-record one hundred home runs at Oklahoma State University. He was drafted initially by the Montreal Expos but held out for, among other things, a shot at playing in the big leagues right away. Texas signed him for a $150,000 signing bonus and the major-league minimum salary of $60,000 a year with a second-year option for $172,000. All the Rangers promised Incaviglia was a shot at the big leagues, and he made the most of it.

Witt had been the Rangers' first-round draft choice the year before. He was a hard-throwing right-hander who, pitching for the University of Oklahoma, once struck out seventeen against the University of Texas. He went to the minor leagues for a year and didn't win a single game, but after working with pitching coach Tom House, the Rangers decided to take a chance on him in '86. Witt and Incaviglia were two of a half dozen rookies who broke camp with the Rangers and would help cast the Rangers as pennant contenders. Pitchers Mitch Williams and Edwin Correa, along with Witt, were dubbed "Witt and Wild" by columnist Randy Galloway, a reference to a nearby water theme park.

Incaviglia finished his first season of pro ball with thirty home runs and 88 RBIs. Larry Parrish and Pete O'Brien combined for fifty-one home runs and 184 RBIs. Witt was wild—he led the league in wild pitches, with twenty-two—but finished with twelve wins. Williams recorded eight wins and the same number of saves. Attendance hit a new all-time franchise record, with almost 1.7 million. By season's end, baseball pundits were tabbing the Rangers as a team to watch and a possible pennant winner for the '87 season. All this after two consecutive last -place finishes.

The Rangers ended the season with a promotion in which the players gave fans the jerseys off their backs. Valentine got hold of a microphone to deliver an impassioned thank-you speech to the fans; the Rangers had drawn almost 1.7 million fans that year. "You ain't seen nothing yet!" Valentine bellowed.

The crowd went wild.

SOME DIVIDED LOYALTIES

Neither the Rangers nor the Astros gave their fans much to go wild about over the next two years. The Astros, following their dramatic playoff appearance in 1986, slumped. Attendance dwindled, dropped and sometimes fell as low as four thousand or so fans who were swallowed by the cavernous Astrodome, where you could not only hear the crack of the bat but also, it seemed, a foul tip.

The one time the fans showed up in anything resembling droves was when Ryan pitched. The forty-one-year-old Ryan, often described at this time as being in the twilight of his career, led the league in ERA with a 2.79 mark, but he lost twice as many games as he won, going 8-16. That was the second-most losses in the league; teammate Dave Knepper was the frustrated leader in that dubious category.

Mike Scott was the team leader in wins, with sixteen. Davis, Doran, Hatcher and Bass continued to play well, but it all translated into a 76-86 record, twenty games worse than the previous year. The old gang was breaking up. Forty-year-old Jose Cruz was released unceremoniously and signed with the Yankees, though he would return to the Astros as a coach and become a fixture in Astros history along with Dierker and Ryan and, like those two, would have his jersey number retired by the team.

The Astros rebounded a bit the next season, and Ryan went 12-11 with a still respectable ERA of 3.52. He kept flirting with no-hitters. In April, pitching against Philadelphia, he took a no-hitter into the ninth inning but lost it on a single by Mike Schmidt with one out. That marked the third time in a row that Ryan had taken a no-hitter into the ninth only to end up with a one-hitter. He won his 100th game as an Astro, becoming the second pitcher in history to win one hundred games in each league.

To show his appreciation, Astros owner John McMullen offered Ryan a 20 percent pay cut. Ryan was Major League Baseball's first million-dollar player when he signed with the Astros, and he stayed at that salary his whole time in Houston. Part of it had to do with the fact that he was plying his trade close to home and was able to spend time with his family in Alvin during the season.

"I would have been perfectly content to do another year at a million dollars," he wrote in *Miracle Man*. "Again, no raise for nine years was not an issue with me because of the benefits that outweighed everything else."

Ryan had 4,775 strikeouts and knew that, barring injury, he would hit a milestone previously thought unreachable: 5,000 strikeouts. A physical fitness fanatic, he still felt strong and capable of pitching one, maybe two, more year(s). He told the Astros, "No, thanks" to the pay cut. Angels' owner Gene Autry, with whom Ryan had remained good friends, was interested in bringing him back to Los Angeles. The San Francisco Giants were interested, and so were the Tokyo Swallows, who sent representatives to visit the Ryans at their ranch.

What really got Ryan's attention was when Tom Grieve called and expressed interest. Grieve said later that he was just testing the waters because he didn't think Houston would let him get away, but Houston did, and Ryan signed with the Rangers because he liked and trusted Grieve, Valentine and club president Mike Stone.

"Money was not the determining factor," Ryan told the Rangers' triumvirate. "I'm a die-hard Texan, so if we can hammer out a few details, I want to stay in Texas." The details got hammered out, and Nolan Ryan became a Texas Ranger. Truly, the Astros' loss would turn out be very much the Rangers' gain in ways none could have imagined at the time.

A lot of baseball fans in Texas might pull for both major-league teams in varying degrees during the course of any season. It's a safe bet that in 2005, when the Astros became the first major-league team from Texas to play in a World Series, Houston fans outnumbered Ranger fans. Six years later, after the Rangers played in two consecutive series, Ranger fans were in the majority. Make no mistake about it, though: both teams have significant numbers of die-hard fans who could never divide their loyalty, even with—or maybe *especially* with—another team from Texas.

Willie Wells was a Rangers fan. He stayed close to the game after retiring from the Negro Leagues and even managed an Austin Little League team in

1974. Sportswriter Donn Rogosin looked Wells up when he was a doctoral candidate in American civilization at the University of Texas. He found out about Wells by reading Robert Peterson's pioneering history of the Negro Leagues, *Only the Ball Was White*. Once, while talking to him with a Rangers' game on in the background, the announcer described Willie Randolph of the Yankees hitting the first pitch thrown to him. "Damn," Wells said. "Everybody knows Randolph is a first-ball hitter."

Wells lived simply and, by most accounts, in relative poverty after he returned to Austin following retirement from the Negro Leagues. Reporters sometimes came around, wanting to talk about his days in baseball. He said he'd had a beautiful career, and the money had actually been pretty good—about $25,000 a year for playing ball for twelve months. Asked about his chances of ever getting into Cooperstown, Wells was optimistic. "I think they'll put more of us in there," he said. "Just let me see it while I'm living."

When pressed about the issue, Wells said it didn't really matter what he thought about it but what other people thought of him as a player. "The sportswriters think so, but it's hard for me to say. I just loved to play. It's such an intelligent game. You learn so much about the character of people. I wouldn't take a million dollars for all the experiences I had with those fellows."

Congressman, J.J. "Jake" Pickle, who represented Texas's tenth congressional district for more than thirty years, wrote to baseball commissioner Bowie Kuhn in 1980, urging him and the selection committee to take a close look at Wells's records, but that was part of the problem; statistics from the Negro Leagues were incomplete, and their reliability varied from league to league, team to team and source to source. The career of even the most mediocre of white major leaguers can usually be traced all the way to Class D ball, but Negro League records didn't survive nearly so neat and intact. Estimates of Wells's career batting average ranged from .364 to .319, but no one who ever saw him play disputed the fact that he was one of the best shortstops they ever saw.

Rube Foster was inducted into the Hall of Fame in Cooperstown in 1981, but Wells died in 1988 at his home in Austin without receiving that recognition. Two years later, Smokey Joe Williams was inducted into the Hall of Fame, almost fifty years after his death. At a ceremony honoring him at the polo grounds in 1950, Williams was asked if he felt any bitterness about being barred from the Major Leagues for so many years because of his race. Williams said he did not. "The important thing is that the long fight is over," he said. "I praise the Lord I've lived to see this day."

While fans in Texas pull for either the Astros or the Rangers—or both—most of them have other loyalties within the state. They pull for their sons' or daughters' Little League teams or high school teams, and they are likely to be fans of either their alma maters or the local college team. The 1990s were a time of change in college baseball in Texas as one legend retired at the University of Texas (Cliff Gustafson) only to be replaced by another legend (Augie Garrido). The Southwest Conference (SWC) disbanded, and Texas, A&M, Texas Tech and Baylor joined the Big 12 Conference. The balance of power shifted in that decade. Though Texas remained a powerhouse, the Longhorns weren't automatically penciled in as the conference champion every year. Other teams battled for a conference championship instead of "second place behind conference champion Texas."

Arkansas tied Texas A&M for the SWC title in 1989, a year in which the Razorbacks and Texas both advanced to the College World Series in Omaha, Nebraska. Texas beat Arkansas twice in the SWC tournament and qualified for regionals despite losing to A&M in the conference finals. UT swept its regional tournament and advanced to the College World Series, where it knocked off Long Beach State, the University of Miami and LSU before losing to Wichita State in the finals. Arkansas tied for fifth at Omaha.

Texas won the next two conference titles. Texas A&M won the conference title in 1993, followed by TCU in '94 and Texas Tech in '95. Fittingly, perhaps, Texas won the last SWC baseball championship in 1996. Texas Tech, under coach Larry Hays, won the first Big 12 championship in 1997.

That year marked the last year that Gustafson coached at UT, stepping aside as the NCAA Division I all-time leader in victories, with 1,427. He was replaced by Augie Garrido, who had built his own dynasty at California State University–Fullerton, where his teams won three national titles. Texas knew Garrido well, having lost the championship game of the 1984 College World Series, 3–2, to his Fullerton team.

On the high school level, longtime powerhouses like Duncanville, Houston Bellaire and Lubbock Monterey maintained strong programs, but like the SWC and Big 12 Conferences, the joy was spread out a little more evenly as teams from Round Rock, Arlington and Fort Bend Elkins challenged for a spot in the Class 5A Division of the University Interscholastic League (UIL) state tournament. Under the UIL's classification system, which puts schools in a classification based on enrollment, smaller schools like Forney, Coahoma, Holliday and Weimar also earned the right to be known as state powerhouses.

Texas high school baseball players continued to find their way to college and professional programs. The state seemed especially adept at turning

Kerry Wood, like Clemens, Clyde and Ryan, first drew attention as a high school phenom.

out hard-throwing pitchers of the David Clyde, Roger Clemens and Nolan Ryan mold. Every year, it seemed, the next Ryan or Clemens was rumored to be pitching for one Texas high school or another.

In 1990, Todd Van Poppel was the guy everybody was talking about. As a senior for Arlington Martin, Poppel had an 11-3 record and a 0.87 ERA. The Atlanta Braves were set to take him, but Poppel assured them he would not sign, so they went with their next pick: Chipper Jones. The Oakland Athletics took Poppel and also another Texas pitcher, Kirk Dressendorfer from UT. Injuries derailed Poppel's career, and he retired from baseball with a 40-52 record.

Five years later, Kerry Wood, who grew up five miles from the Rangers' ballpark, emerged as the state's most dominating pitcher, and he also had a Ryan-like fastball to go with the hype. He started out as an undersized freshman shortstop at Irving MacArthur High School but started fooling around on the pitcher's mound after a six-inch growth spurt as a sophomore. As a pitcher, he modeled his motion and demeanor after his two favorite pitchers: Nolan Ryan and Roger Clemens. He first caught the attention of big-league scouts in 1994 in a game against Arlington Martin. The scouts were there to see another high school phenom, Ben Grieve, the son of former Rangers' general manager Tom Grieve. The showdown between the two hot shots was a draw. Wood struck out Grieve the first time he faced him, but Grieve took him deep in his next at-bat.

Wood transferred to Grand Prairie High School for his senior year, and now he was the one the scouts were coming to see. The Chicago Cubs drafted him in the fourth round of the amateur draft in 1995, one slot behind Jose Cruz Jr. of Rice University. In a playoff series against Round Rock, Wood pitched seventeen innings, which drew the attention—and the ire—of the Cubs' brass. The club had Wood undergo a series of medical tests and signed him after doctors gave him a clean bill of health. He was the National League Rookie of the Year in 1998, bursting onto the national scene in a big way on May 6. Facing a good Astros team, Wood tied Roger Clemens's major-league record by striking out twenty batters in a nine-inning game. He missed the next season after having "Tommy John" surgery to repair his right elbow but returned the next season.

Since then, Wood has shown flashes of brilliance, but he has been plagued his whole career by arm problems and other sometimes nagging, sometimes serious injuries. Given all that he has had to overcome, Wood deserves credit for persevering and becoming a well-rounded pitcher with a solid big-league career instead of another "can't miss" prospect who did. After being traded by Chicago to Cleveland and then to the Yankees, Wood is back with the Cubs as a relief pitcher.

Nolan Ryan found himself in that odd position of making history every time he stepped on the mound. As the all-time strikeout leader, the record moved up a notch every time he struck somebody out. He already had the record for the most no-hitters, with five, and had come ever so close so many times to pushing that number to six. The other numbers are so gaudy that it's easy to forget that he had twelve one-hitters and eighteen two-hitters; a break or two here and there and the man could have been in double-digit no-hitters.

On July 11, 1990, Ryan finally got his sixth no-hitter. This one came at the expense of the Oakland Athletics, whom he baffled with his change-up as much as he overpowered them with his famous fastball. His back was bothering him, which kept some of the mustard off his fastball, but by the seventh inning, Oakland hitters said he was throwing every bit of ninety-five miles per hour.

Nolan Ryan being carried off the field after his seventh no-hitter. *Associated Press.*

The fans were almost delirious by the time the ninth inning rolled around, but this one didn't slip away. Ryan struck out pinch-hitter Ken Phelps to open the ninth, his fourteenth strikeout of the night. All fourteen went down swinging, a testament to how well the change-up was working. Shortstop Jeff Huson made a nice play on a slow roller for the second out, and Willie Randolph flied out to Reuben Sierra in right for the final out. At forty-three, Ryan became the oldest pitcher in major-league history to throw a no-hitter and the first to throw one for three different teams.

"I've been close before so I know what the disappointment is like," Ryan said after the game. "When I went out there for the ninth, I told myself that if I was going to get beat, it was only going to be with my best pitches."

Two weeks later, Ryan could again be found inserting himself into the record books, this time adding his name to the list of pitchers with three hundred victories in an 11–3 Rangers win over the Brewers in Milwaukee. Pitching with a stress fracture in his lower back, he left the game with two outs in the seventh after giving up one earned run and six hits. Brad Arnsberg got the final four outs for the most historic save of his career, and the Rangers made sure of things in the top of the ninth with a home run by Incaviglia and a grand slam by Julio Franco, which more than atoned for two errors he had made in the fourth inning.

Less than a year later, on May 1, 1992, Ryan, now forty-four, fashioned another masterpiece: his seventh no-hitter, a 3–0 victory over the Toronto Blue Jays. Ryan was, pitching coach Tom House said, "in a zone where normal people don't go." He missed a perfect game by issuing two walks on full counts and struck out sixteen Blue Jays. "They just got in the way of a train," Huson said. The last strikeout—a ninety-three-mile-per-hour fastball past a swinging Roberto Alomar in the ninth—caused another adjustment in the major-league record books. Ryan's exploits were taking on a freakish quality, something Gerry Fraley captured in his game story the next day for the *Dallas Morning News*.

"To grasp the magnitude of what Ryan accomplished, consider his final victim. When Ryan pitched his first two no-hitters with California in 1973, his second baseman was Sandy Alomar. Roberto Alomar is Sandy Alomar's twenty-three-year-old son who as a child asked Ryan to help him become a pitcher."

The sixth and seventh no-hitters made Ryan the only pitcher in history to pitch a no-hitter in four separate decades.

Houston fans had mixed feelings about Ryan's superman act in Arlington. Few people faulted Ryan for not accepting a salary cut to stay with the Astros, and the fans he made and headlines he garnered provided a source for much wailing and gnashing of teeth in the Bayou City. He was their hometown boy made good, but John McMullen forced him to leave home. So he had moved next door and added new records and a new layer to his legend.

The hometown team wasn't giving the Houston fans a lot to cheer about, struggling to get above the .500 mark from 1990 to 1992. One bright spot was the play of their 1987 first-round draft choice Craig Biggio. He was a catcher and everything a catcher is supposed to be except for big—he was listed at five feet, eleven inches and 180 pounds but appeared smaller—and he was also something that catchers usually aren't, which is very fast. He hit .344 in the minors and was called up in 1988 and became Houston's full-time catcher the following year. By 1991, he had been named to the National League all-star team as a catcher, but manager Art Howe convinced him to switch to second base for the 1992 season. Astros management wanted to save Biggio's speed—he was stealing twenty to twenty-five bases a year—and worried that the rigors of catching would sap the speed before its time. Biggio gamely said he'd give it a try and made the 1992 all-star team as a second baseman, the only time a player has been an all-star at each of those two positions.

Another glimmer of hope was the acquisition of Jeff Bagwell from the Boston Red Sox. Bagwell was a New England kid and grew up as a Red

Craig Biggio came up as a catcher but was moved to second in hopes of prolonging his career. *Houston Astros.*

Sox fan who idolized Carl Yastrzemski. But Bagwell's prospects of playing in front of friends and family at Fenway Park were bleak. Bagwell hit better than .300 in the Red Sox minor-league system, and without a lot of power; he hit just six home runs in more than 750 minor-league at-bats. Wade Boggs had held down third base, Bagwell's position, at Fenway for many years and in Hall of Fame fashion. Boggs would depart in 1992, but the Red Sox had a couple other prospects at third base. They needed relief pitching for a playoff run, and so they dealt Bagwell to the Astros for thirty-six-year-old reliever Larry Andersen.

As bad as the Joe Morgan trade was, this one was every bit as good, the best one the team ever made. Andersen left the Red Sox for free agency after helping Boston into the playoffs, but Bagwell hit .294 with eighty-two RBIs and fifteen home runs and was the 1991 Rookie of the Year. Die-hard Boston fans—is there any other kind?—still call Bagwell-for-Andersen the second worst trade in club history, ranking only behind the trade that sent Babe Ruth to the Yankees.

It's good to be smart, but it helps to be lucky, too. Bagwell was a decent prospect—.300 hitters usually are—but Ken Caminti was entrenched at third base for the Astros. Glenn Davis was gone, so Bagwell was moved to

Jeff Bagwell's peculiar stance produced big results. *Andrew Woolley.*

first base, where he soon rounded into Gold Glove form. Bagwell was a bit of an experiment at first, but it worked early and for a long time. Biggio and Bagwell both played in every game of the 1992 season, a feat they would repeat in 1996.

Bagwell experimented with and changed his stance from time to time during his first years with the Astros, something he had picked up from Yastrzemski. Tony Gwynn suggested he pick a stance and stay with it. The stance he picked was one of the most unique of all time. He crouched at the plate, legs spread almost impossibly wide, and had a hitch in his swing that made hitting instructors all over the country cringe. If all that wasn't enough, he stepped *away* from the pitch instead of into it—the dreaded "step in the bucket" stride—and planted his front foot when he swung. And when he swung— usually as hard as he could—from this exaggerated position, the ball often went great distances. Tom Verducci of *Sports Illustrated* described his stance as looking like "a game of Twister breaking out in the batter's box."

About the time he switched to that stance and that swing—1994—was about the same time Bagwell served notice that pitchers should worry a great deal about pitching to him. In 1994, Bagwell put together the kind of season that Ring Lardner or a writer of juvenile sports fiction might have created, but the numbers would have been considered too outlandish to be believable. Bagwell had four hundred plate appearances but drove in 116 runs, scored 104 and hit 39 home runs—and, oh yeah, he hit .369. Voters had an easy time choosing him as National League MVP. "Crazy stuff happened that year," Bagwell said. "Every pitch I was looking for I got. And when I got it, I didn't miss it. It was ridiculous."

Bagwell's season ended prematurely, but so did everyone else's. Bagwell's peculiar stance had one drawback: it made it hard to get out of the way of pitches that drifted too far inside. His 1993 season had been cut short when a pitch from the Phillies' Ben Rivera broke his hand. The same thing happened in 1994, on August 10, just two days before yet another players' strike ended Major League Baseball for the year and canceled the World Series for the first time in ninety years. This was baseball's eighth work stoppage, and it was a doozy, the longest and most acrimonious in the history of the game or, indeed, any other major North American sports league. Bagwell had picked a bad year to have a good season, as had several other players like Ken Griffey Jr. and Tony Gwynn, who were poised to make a run at some of the most hallowed records in baseball history.

In a strange year for baseball, it was fitting, perhaps, that the Texas Rangers found themselves in the strangest situation when the strike ended the worst pennant race in history. The Rangers were ten games under .500 but led a revamped American League West Division. Last-place teams in other divisions had better records than the Rangers, who were in the process of reinventing themselves again. Valentine had been let go in 1992, and Nolan Ryan retired in 1993, giving the record books a chance to breathe and catch up. The final strikeout tally: 5,714.

One thing Nolan Ryan never had was a perfect game, but Kenny Rogers pitched one on July 28, squeezing into the record books as the twelfth pitcher in major-league history to not allow a hit or a base runner through nine innings. Rogers didn't have the pedigree of Ryan. He played right field for one year of high school baseball so, naturally, the Rangers drafted him as a pitcher in the thirty-ninth round of the 1982 draft, almost as an afterthought after a scout saw him make a good throw from right field. He worked his way up through the minor leagues one rung at a time: on-the-job training. Rogers didn't know how to throw a curveball when he signed; couldn't pitch out of the stretch. Didn't have a clue. Against the Angels that day, he didn't have to pitch out of the stretch.

Rogers struck out eight and went to a three-ball count just six times against the Angels. Chili Davis hit a hard liner to left in the eighth, the most solid

Ivan Rodriguez was a mainstay for the Rangers and one of the best catchers in the game.

contact an Angel hitter made against him. Rex Hudler hit a soft blooper to center to lead off the ninth that rookie centerfielder Rusty Greer nabbed with a sensational diving catch.

"Even if I didn't catch it, I was going to give it my best shot," Greer said. It was the first perfect game in Rangers history and came ten years after Mike

Witt pitched a perfect game against the Rangers on the last day of the 1984 season. Rogers also became the first left-hander to throw a perfect game in the American League.

Though the 1994 Rangers will always be known as the team that went 52-62 but finished in first place in the American League West, the nucleus of a good ball club was falling into place. The catcher for Rogers's perfect game was Ivan Rodriguez, a rocket-armed twenty-two-year-old from Puerto Rico, where he often played against Ranger teammate Juan Gonzalez. Signed by the Rangers when he was just sixteen, Rodriguez was playing minor-league ball at seventeen and was the Rangers' starting catcher by the time he was nineteen. Almost from the time he first stepped onto a major-league diamond, he was described as the best catcher in baseball since Johnny Bench. By 1994, he was leading the league in throwing out runners trying to steal, a category he would dominate for years to come. He hit .298 that year, the highest among major-league catchers, and hit sixteen home runs.

Countryman Gonzales had nineteen home runs for Texas and both first baseman Will Clark (.329) and Greer (.314) hit better than .300 for a team that was becoming known as a murderer's row of sluggers. Well-traveled home run specialist and muscle man Jose Canseco also showed up on the Rangers' roster and was the American League Comeback Player of the Year, with thirty-one home runs and ninety RBIs. He also had a fly ball bounce off his head and into the stands for a home run. Later, Canseco's presence on the Rangers would cast a shadow over the team and many of its stars.

In the short term, the strike of 1994 overshadowed everything else that happened in baseball that year. Fans

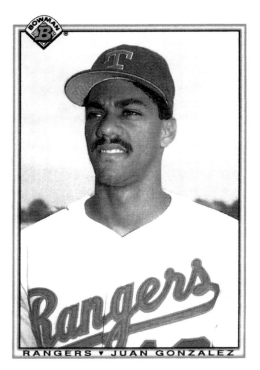

RANGERS ▼ JUAN GONZALEZ

On a Rangers team known for sluggers, Juan Gonzalez was the best known.

137

acted with outrage and disappointment. Many called it the biggest threat to Major League Baseball's survival since the Black Sox Scandal of 1919. Attendance plummeted by 20 percent across major-league parks in 1995, which were often the scene of protests and angry banners held up by many of the fans who did return to major-league parks. The strike seemed to hang over everything in 1995.

The Rangers took the opportunity to clean house after the 1994 season. Grieve was fired and replaced by Doug Melvin, who fired Kennedy and brought in Johnny Oates to manage. Canseco, a designated hitter with a $5 million salary, was dealt to the Red Sox. The '95 Rangers challenged for a playoff spot well into September but faltered down the stretch and finished third in the four-team division. More than twenty years after coming to Texas, the Rangers had not yet seriously challenged for a berth in postseason play, the '94 season notwithstanding.

In Houston, owner Drayton McLane, reeling from the strike and what it had done to the team's financial bottom line, shipped away Caminit and five other players to the Padres for, among others, Derek Bell. Given that he would become a key contributor to Houston, and his last name started with "B," he became, along with Bagwell and Biggio, part of what was called the "Killer Bs." Bagwell was lost for the last part of the season after his hand was broken (again) by an (another) inside pitch. The team went into a tailspin without Bagwell and never fully recovered, finishing with a 76-68 record. The Astros went 82-80 in 1996 but failed again to make the playoffs.

DREAMS OF A TEXAS WORLD SERIES

I f there was ever going to be an All-Texas World Series—Rangers versus Astros—1994 was probably the best chance of that happening. The Astros were just a half game out of first place when the season ended prematurely. In the late 1990s, hope was born anew when both Texas teams made the playoffs, but the two dominant teams of the 1990s—the Atlanta Braves in the National League and the Yankees in the American League—deferred that particular diamond dream.

The 1996 Rangers team, bolstered by a monstrous MVP year from Juan Gonzalez, finally made a postseason appearance for the first time in franchise history. Gonzalez walloped 47 home runs, drove in 144 runs and hit .314. Greer had blossomed into a .332 hitter and added 19 home runs and eighty-six RBIs. "Pudge" Rodriguez, as he was generally known, hit an even .300, threw out nearly half the runners who tried to steal on him and made sure others never got the chance by picking off runners at first and third, right and left, sometimes from his knees. Shortstop Kevin Elster, named the American League's Comeback Player of the Year, added 24 home runs and ninety-nine RBIs. Five pitchers notched double-digit wins, led by Bobby Witt and Ken Hill, with sixteen apiece, and Roger Pavlik and Darren Oliver, with fourteen. Closer Mike Hennemann anchored the bullpen with thirty-one saves. It all added up to a 90-72 record and an American League West Division title.

The Rangers acquired John Burkett from Florida for the playoff run, but Burkett would stay with the Rangers for three more years and be a key part of the team's subsequent playoff appearances. He was the winning pitcher in the Rangers' first-ever playoff game and victory, 6–2 over the Yankees in Yankee Stadium in game one of the National League Division Series (NLDS). The Rangers broke it open in the fifth on a three-run home run by Gonzalez and a two-run shot by Dean Palmer.

Gonzales homered again in the second inning of game two for a 1–0 Ranger lead and tagged a three-run bomb in the third that made the score Gonzales, 4, Yankees, 1. But the Yankees chipped away at the lead and tied it in the eighth on an RBI single by Cecil Fielder. The game went to extra innings, and the Rangers put the leadoff man on in the tenth, eleventh and twelfth innings, but the Yankees won it in the bottom of the twelfth.

Back in Texas for game three, the first home playoff game in franchise history, the Rangers sent Oliver to the mound. He gave up a home run to Bernie Williams in the first but settled down quickly and completely; the Yankees wouldn't score again until the ninth. By that time, Gonzalez— "Señor October," as he was being called—had hit his fourth home run of the series, and Rodriguez had doubled home a run, appropriate since he had set a major-league record for most doubles by a catcher, with forty-four. He and Gonzales were simply continuing what they had done during the regular season. But the Yankees got two in the ninth and won, 3–2, on an RBI single by Mariano Duncan.

Kenny Rogers, who had parlayed his success and perfect game notoriety with the Rangers into a lucrative contract with the Yankees, started game four against Witt, but the Rangers chased him early. Gonzalez came to bat in the third inning and hit his fifth home run of the series, which, coupled with an unearned run later in the inning, put the Rangers up, 4–0. The lead turned out to be surmountable as the Yankees scored three in the fourth and eventually won it on Fielder's RBI single in the eighth; a Bernie Williams home run in the ninth made it a 6–4 final and chased the Rangers from their first playoff series.

In 1997, Astros owner Drayton McLane, president Tal Smith and general manager Gerry Hunsicker tabbed Larry Dierker to be the next manager of the Astros. Dierker, of course, had fashioned a fine major-league career with the Astros but had become the Astros' radio and TV announcer in 1979.

He was good at it, too. Funny as hell. A real card. Knew his baseball. Great man for the job—the broadcast job, not the manager's job. The thing was, in many people's minds, Dierker had been in the broadcast booth a lot longer than he had pitched in the Major Leagues. Now he was known for wearing Hawaiian shirts and showing a wry sense of humor.

Dierker was a sharp contrast to the man he replaced as manager, Terry Collins, who was as high strung as Dierker was laid back. Dierker filled out his staff with former Astros like Bill Virdon, the winningest manager in Astros history, as bench coach and longtime fan favorite Jose Cruz as first base coach. Vern Ruhle was brought in as the pitching coach. Together with a lineup backed by Bagwell, Biggio and Bell, the Astros made a run at the title and, to the dismay of naysayers everywhere, won it.

Bagwell paced the Astros at the plate, becoming the first Astro to reach 40 home runs, finishing with 43 and 135 doubles. He had also learned to take pitches and was among the league leaders in walks; he even stole thirty-one bases. That marked the first time that a first baseman hit 30 home runs and stole thirty bases in a season. Biggio, batting leadoff, hit .309 and stole forty-seven bases. The Astros and Rangers also faced each other for the first time in a game that counted as Major League Baseball instituted interleague play. The Rangers took that first meeting, 8–1.

The National League Central was called Comedy Central mostly because the play wasn't that, you know, good. The Astros stayed in contention despite hovering around the .500 mark for most of the season but clinched the pennant eleven years to the day after Mike Scott had clinched a division title with a no-hitter. On this day, Darrell Kile pitched a four-hitter for the Astros against the Cubs.

That put Houston in the NLDS against the Atlanta Braves and their pitching juggernaut of Greg Maddux, John Smoltz and Tom Glavine. Maddux came out on the winning end of a 2–1 pitching duel against Kyle in the opener. The second game was a 13–3 Atlanta blowout, and Smoltz pitched a three-hitter in game three, sweeping Houston from the playoffs. Bagwell, Biggio and Bell, the Killer Bs, combined for just two hits against Atlanta pitching.

The 1997 division title finally got the Astros over the hump after three consecutive second-place finishes, but Dierker and the Astros set out to prove in 1998 that the previous year wasn't a fluke. They did that. A franchise always known for its pitching, with its offense considered an afterthought, this Astros team pounded the ball and led the league in runs scored, with 874, and RBIs, with 818. Moises Alou clouted 38 home runs and drove in

124 runs, while Bagwell hit 34 dingers and drove in 111. Bell was a .314 hitter with 22 home runs and 109 RBIs. Houston had six players with double-digit home runs and eight players with ten or more steals. Biggio was now the best leadoff hitter in baseball. He led the team with a .325 average and set a club record with 210 hits. He became the first player in major-league history since Texan Tris Speaker in 1912 to hit 50 doubles and steal fifty bases.

While the Astros were making their own kind of news at the plate, the big story in baseball was the home run chase of Roger Maris's single-season record of sixty-one home runs, set in 1961, a year before the Astros were born. Mark McGwire finished the season with seventy home runs, and Sammy Sosa had sixty-six. Their well-chronicled chase of the record was credited with bringing fans back to major-league ballparks after the bitterness and acrimony of the 1994 strike.

If Houston fans had any doubt about management's intention of reaching the World Series, they were dispelled when the Astros signed the "Big Unit," six-foot-ten Randy Johnson, for the final two months of the season. Johnson was magnificent for Houston down the stretch, winning his first game as an Astro against Pittsburgh, shutting out the Phillies, outdueling Maddux and shutting out Cincinnati and St. Louis. Thanks in part to Johnson, who continued to get plenty of help from his Astro teammates at the plate, Houston won more than one hundred games for the first time in his history, finishing with a 102-60 record. Nobody laughed when Dierker was named the National League Manager of the Year.

That put Houston in the NLDS against the San Diego Padres, who had won ninety-eight games in the National League West. Johnson was the go-to guy in game one, and he pitched magnificently, but Kevin Brown was even better, setting a playoff record with sixteen strikeouts in a 2–1 Padre victory.

In game two, Houston got three RBIs from Bagwell and a home run from Bell for a 4–2 lead, with ace closer Billy Wagner, whom some said threw as hard as Nolan Ryan in his prime, set to close the deal in the ninth. Jim Leyritz stunned the Astrodome crowd with a two-run home run in the ninth to tie the game. Billy Spiers, not mentioned as a future Hall of Famer like his better-known teammates, was the hero with a game-winning RBI single in the tenth.

With a day off between each of the first three games to accommodate the TV schedule, Kevin Brown took the mound again in game three against Mike Hampton. The two dueled each other through four scoreless innings, but Leyritz, doing his best Reggie Jackson and Juan Gonzalez impersonations, had one of only three Padre hits, a game-winning home run in a 2–1 Houston loss.

Johnson was back on the mound for Houston in game four, but the Padres' Sterling Hitchcock and the San Diego bullpen outpitched him, holding the Astros to just three hits in a 2–1 loss. The season was over several weeks sooner than the Astros had anticipated.

Basically, the same thing happened again to Houston in 1999, the last year the team would play its home games in the Astrodome. The former "Eighth Wonder of the World" had given rise to a new cliché: a shell of its former self. McMullen had been disenchanted with the Astrodome in his final days as owner and even tried to sell the team and franchise to a group that would move it to Washington, D.C. National League owners blocked the move, so McMullen was stuck with the team until he sold it to McLane in 1993.

Like McMullen, he had tried to move the team out of Houston for want of a new facility and almost succeeded, but the move was delayed at the last minute, and Houston voters indicated that they approved of a new stadium.

A new field, Enron Field, a baseball-only facility, was in the works by the end of the decade. The season was anticipated as sort of a celebration of the team's and the Astrodome's history—and maybe there would be a victory lap as the Astros tried to break through to the other side of the playoffs' first round. The season turned out to be dramatic in ways that no one could have anticipated when the season began.

Jose Lima predicted that he would win twenty games in '99; he won twenty-one. Hampton went him one better, going 22-4, but Alou missed the season with a knee injury, and new catcher Mitch Meluskey was out after ten games with a shoulder injury. Bagwell firmly planted himself in the Houston record books, eclipsing Jimmy Wynn's team record for most home runs (224) and walks, with 149, as part of a season in which he hit 42 home runs, drove in 128 runs, scored 130 and hit .304. Biggio was up to his old tricks, banging out 188 hits, including a club-record 56 doubles, while stealing twenty-eight bases and cementing his reputation as one of the best defensive second basemen in the game.

Despite some early injuries, things were basically going great for the Astros until June 13, when Dierker suffered a seizure on the field; only emergency brain surgery saved his life. Dierker returned to the dugout after the all-star break, but injuries continued to plague the team. Dierker said he thought he did a better job of managing that year, with all the injuries and real-life drama to contend with, than he did in 1998, when he was Manager of the Year.

Somehow, whether through Dierker's inspiration or the sometimes inspired play of otherwise unheralded role players, the Astros continued to

Mike Hampton bolstered a strong Astro pitching staff with twenty-two wins in 1999.

hold their own in a division race that went down to the last day of the season and the last regular season game the Astros would ever play in the dome.

Houston made it a memorable and happy occasion, beating Los Angeles, 9–1, and clinching the division crown, thus avoiding a one-game playoff to determine its playoff fate. Hampton got his twenty-second win of the year for the Astros, Ward drove in three runs with a bases-loaded double in the first and, by and large, a good time was had by all in the dome, which was destined to see at least a couple more playoff games.

Facing the Braves again in the NLDS, Shane Reynolds came out on top in a match-up against Maddux. Daryle Ward homered to give Houston the lead in the sixth, and Caminit salted it away with a three-run shot as part of a 6–1 Houston win. It was the first time Houston held a lead in a playoff series since 1986, but Kevin Millwood evened the series the next day with a one-hitter in a 5–1 Braves win.

Hampton took the mound for game three against Maddux, and his teammates staked him to a run lead before Brian Jordan's home run made it a 3–2 game in Atlanta's favor. Billy Spiers tied it for Houston with an RBI single, and the game went into extra innings. Houston loaded the bases with nobody out in the bottom of the tenth against Atlanta closer John Rocker, but he shut down the rally due in no small part to shortstop Walt Weiss, who made the play of the postseason with a diving stop of a hard liner up the middle and a pinpoint throw home in time for the out. Jordan hit a two-run double in the twelfth for a 5–3 win that would haunt the Astros and Dierker for a while.

Atlanta jumped to a 7–0 lead in game four and appeared ready to break out the champagne when Houston began battling back on a solo homer by Tony Eusebio and three-run blast by Caminit in the eighth. Caminit almost tied it in the ninth with two outs and one on, but his long drive to center came up a few feet short, and Houston once again watched Atlanta celebrate while the Astros were left to ponder yet again what might have been.

Talk of an All-Texas World Series died in the first round of the playoffs in 1998 and 1999. With the Astros winning division crowns in the National League, the Rangers, under no-nonsense manager Johnny Oates, won the 1998 and 1999 American League West titles but were bounced from the playoffs in three straight games by the New York Yankees both years. In a football-crazy state, the Rangers often won (and lost) by scores that are more usually associated with football.

Leading the hit parade for the Rangers was Juan Gonzalez, who from 1995 through 1998 had 514 RBIs in 511 games. He was the American League MVP in 1996 and again in 1998; teammate Ivan Rodriguez would win it in 1999. Gonzalez had more than 100 RBIs by the all-star break in 1998, including a major-league record 35 in April, and finished with 157 RBIs and forty-five home runs. Like Bagwell and Biggio in Houston, and unlike his record-setting home run barrage against the Yankees in 1996, Gonzalez went just 1 for 12 against the Yankees in the American League Division Series (ALDS). In the 1999 playoffs, another sweep by the Yankees, Gonzalez's solo home run was the only run the Rangers scored.

Pudge Rodriguez put it all together in 1999, setting a record for most home runs by a catcher, with thirty-five, and also setting a record for catchers by being the first to have more than thirty home runs and 100 RBIs in a single season; he also hit .322, and his twenty-five stolen bases were the fifth most by a catcher in American League history. None of this added up to anything resembling postseason success other than simply getting there.

The Astros returned to postseason play, again briefly, in 2001, fueled by Bagwell and Biggio, of course (Biggio collected his 2,000th hit on May 4), but also, surprisingly, by several young players who were called on after injuries, trades and disappointing play made a shambles of the team Dierker had intended to field.

Ivan "Pudge" Rodriguez was the American League MVP in 1999.

Lance Berkman was a switch-hitter from Austin who played at Rice University before becoming an all-star with the Astros. *Houston Astros.*

Roy Oswalt was called up from the minors in May and promptly went 14-3 with a 2.73 ERA the rest of the way; he didn't see the minor leagues again. Lance Berkman, a switch-hitting outfielder from Rice University by way of Austin, established himself as a full-fledged all-star by hitting .331 and smacking thirty-four home runs. The Astros signed Vinny Castilla when he was released by Tampa Bay, and Castilla contributed twenty-three home runs and eighty-two RBIs.

By August, it all started clicking, and the Astros scratched, clawed and fought their way back into contention. Down one game with three games against the division-leading Cardinals remaining, Houston took two of three from the Cards and earned the right to face, yet again, the dream-killing Atlanta Braves. The Braves did it again, sweeping Houston from the playoffs rather unceremoniously in three games.

Dierker, the fun-loving broadcaster, had become the besieged manager. He had taken his team to the playoffs in four of his five years as manager, but the team's playoff record during that time was 2-12. The laid-back surfer dude snapped at the media following the series and was booed in his own ballpark for walking Barry Bonds while Bonds was in pursuit of the single-season home run record. His moves were questioned, second-guessed and challenged by the media. It didn't take long for Dierker to decide and the Astros to agree, or vice versa, that it was time for Dierker to move on.

"It's been tough, tougher than I anticipated," he said when he stepped down. "I understand looking at this from a player's standpoint. Sometimes, things can get stale. I think I reached that point with this team."

On May 19, 2002, the Astros retired the number forty-nine in honor of Dierker, who was with the Astros for thirty-eight years. As a player, he was second only to Joe Niekro for the most wins in team history and the owner of team records for innings pitched, starts, complete games and shutouts. He was with the team from their hot and humid days at Colt Stadium to the Astrodome to Enron Field, from expansion fodder to something like a perennial playoff contender. More than anybody else, Dierker's life story parallels the history of major-league baseball in Houston.

As for the prospects of an All-Texas World Series, given recent developments, it doesn't look like it will ever happen. The two teams would return to postseason play in the 2000s, and both would make their first-ever World Series appearances, but the harmonic convergence that could have brought us a Lone Star World Series never happened.

MORE THAN A GAME

Willie Wells was inducted into the Baseball Hall of Fame on August 3, 1997. Just as he had predicted, the honor came after his death. His daughter, Stella Wells, found out about the honor on the local news. "I broke down and cried," she told a reporter several days later. "Daddy was right. He just knew he'd get in. He'd tell people, I may be dead, but I'll get in."

Stella Wells spoke on behalf of her father at the induction ceremony in Cooperstown. "To my father, baseball was more than game," she said. "It was a way of life. He understood the importance of applying hard work, wisdom, intelligence, leadership and persistence to his primary goal to win a baseball game."

In October 2004, Wells was reinterred at the Texas State Cemetery in Austin, and a new marker that acknowledged his baseball legacy was unveiled. Former Negro League star and Hall of Famer Buck O'Neil, a longtime friend and supporter of Wells's induction into the Hall of Fame, gave the keynote speech. The choir from Huston-Tillotson College, where Jackie Robinson had served as athletic director after his court-martial at Fort Hood and where Willie Wells enrolled briefly to please his mother, sang "Take Me Out to the Ball Game."

While people had wondered and even doubted if Wells would ever be inducted into the Hall of Fame, Nolan Ryan was expected to be a first-ballot shoo-in somewhere around the time of his 5,000th strikeout and sixth or seventh no-hitter. In 1999, two years after Wells's posthumous induction, Ryan spoke to about fifty thousand people as his Hall of Fame plaque and likeness was unveiled for the ages. He spoke of the God-given gift of throwing

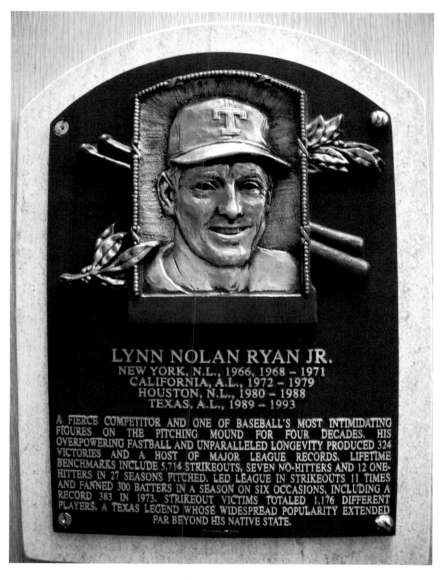

Nolan Ryan's plaque at the Baseball Hall of Fame in Cooperstown, New York. *National Baseball Hall of Fame.*

a baseball, and he spoke long and lovingly of his parents and family and thanked his high school and youth league coaches. He also thanked the man who had noticed him on a high school diamond all those years ago and saw something in him that other's didn't.

"Red Murff, the scout who signed me for the Mets, is here with us today. And I am proud to say that Red is a friend and that Red took more of an interest in me at an early age and, when he saw me at six-two and 140, wasn't discouraged by my build and by the way I threw the baseball as many other scouts were," Ryan said. "And I appreciate the fact that Red spent so much time with me and worked to help me become a better pitcher. Thank you, Red."

Smokey Joe Williams, the original long, lanky Texan with a blazing fastball and a wicked curve, was also inducted into the Hall of Fame in 1997, though with considerably less fanfare. By 2001, eighteen Negro leaguers had been inducted into the Baseball Hall of Fame, including Rube Foster and his half brother, Willie Foster, and Hilton Smith. Lewis Santop and Raleigh "Biz" Mackey were inducted in 2006.

We pause here to remember a player from baseball's early days with the unlikely name of Chicken Wolf, who played for ten years in the American Association, the forerunner of the American League. Wolf holds the distinction for being perhaps the lowest-paid major leaguer in history. In 1882, his rookie year, Louisville paid him a mere $9 a week, a paltry sum even by the standards of the time. What would Chicken Wolf have thought of the $252 million contract that Alex Rodriguez signed with the Texas Rangers in 2001? What would Willie Wells and his fellow Negro leaguers have thought? For that matter, what would Rogers Hornsby or Tris Speaker have thought?

In 2001, most people thought Rangers' owner Tom Hicks was crazy. Even at a time when nine-figure player contracts were treated as everyday sports news, the deal between Alex Rodriguez—"A-Rod," as he was called—raised the bar so high you needed a telescope to spot it. Hicks insisted that A-Rod would be the foundation of many pennant-winning Rangers' teams to come.

Aside from calling into question Hick's sanity, criticism of the deal centered on the fact that Texas had one of the worst pitching staffs in Major League Baseball in the early 2000s. The money paid to Rodriguez could have bought a lot of pitching and maybe allowed the Rangers to keep some stars they had to let go, like Pudge Rodriguez, who became a free agent after the 2002 season and signed with the Florida Marlins. For the Rangers, the Alex Rodriguez years turned out to be a classic case of good news, bad news.

The Texas Rangers paid Alex Rodriguez $252 million, but they finished in last place every year he was with the team.

The good news was that Rodriguez, regarded as one of the two or three best all-around players in the game and one of the best to ever put on a uniform, produced in a big way for the Rangers. In three years with the team, he hit a staggering 156 home runs and drove in 395 runs while hitting at a .305 clip and establishing himself as one of the best defensive shortstops in the game. Despite playing on the league's last-place team, he was named the American League's Most Valuable Player in 2003.

And there's the rub. The Rangers had one of the best, if not the best, players in the Major Leagues, but they finished last for four straight years, including the three years that A-Rod was putting up the best numbers in the game. All the while, the pitching staff struggled with team ERAs of .571 in 2001 and .515 the following year. A-Rod put up some astonishing numbers for the Rangers, but he could not account for five runs a game all by himself.

By the end of the 2003 season, Hicks no longer believed Alex Rodriguez was the warhorse that would lead the Rangers to an American League pennant, and Alex Rodriguez himself realized he could not turn around a team on his own. The Rangers were still on the hook for his salary but believed that getting rid of him would be a case of addition by subtraction. He was dealt to the Yankees for second baseman Alfonsio Soriano and a minor-league prospect. Fairly or unfairly, Ranger fans never really warmed to Rodriguez and for years after he left they blamed him in some fundamental way for the team finishing last every year he was in Texas.

In 2004, their first year without A-Rod in the lineup, the Rangers finally climbed out of the cellar and breathed the not exactly rarefied air of third place in the American League West. Rodriguez was later alleged to have used performance-enhancing drugs (PEDs) when he was with the Rangers, but in that regard, he was far from being the Lone Ranger. Whether named in the "secret" Mitchell Report on steroid and PED use in baseball or named by Jose Canseco in his book about his own and others' use, suspicions were also cast upon fan favorites like Juan Gonzales, Rafael Palmeiro and Pudge Rodriguez. For Ranger fans, it was a dark time. Not only did it appear that their team had little to look forward to, but also the whispers and allegations tainted fond memories of better days gone by.

None of this would seem even remotely real to Chicken Wolf.

———

The Astros, under new manager Jimmy Williams, finished second in the National League Central in 2003. After declining to sign any high-priced free agents in '02, McLane gambled on all-star second baseman Kent Hance

Roy Oswalt came up quickly through Houston's minor-league system to become one of the best pitchers in the National League.

for the '03 season, despite Biggio's presence at second. Biggio offered to switch to center field, and Berkman moved to right.

On June 11 of that year, the Astros authored the most unusual no-hitter in baseball history at one of the most storied venues in baseball: Yankee Stadium. Oswalt, fresh off a stint on the disabled list, started the interleague game but reinjured himself on the second pitch of the second inning. Pete Munro was called in for emergency relief duty. He hit one batter and walked another, and a third reached base on an error, but he got out of the inning without allowing any runs or, more importantly to history, any hits. Kirk Saarloos took over in the fourth, followed by Brad Lidge in the sixth and Octavio Dotel in the eighth. None of them allowed any hits either.

Wagner came on in the ninth to seal the deal and did. When Hideki Matsui hit a grounder to Bagwell at first and he flipped to Wagner covering the bag, Wagner yelled and pumped his fist in the air. Kent looked at him like he had lost his mind. Most of the Astro players had no idea a no-hitter was in progress.

The no-hitter was the tenth in Houston history and rivaled Ken Johnson's no-hitter in a losing effort for the Colt .45s as the most unusual, setting a record for the most pitchers combining on a no-hitter—six—in major-league history. It also marked just the third time the Yankees had ever been no-hit and the first time it happened to them at Yankee Stadium. To their credit and the Astros' appreciation, the Yankee fans gave the Houston pitching sextet a standing ovation.

The Astros contended well into September for the National League Central crown, despite injuries to Oswalt, but faltered badly down the stretch. Going into the final three games of the season against the Brewers, the Astros were tied with the Cubs for first place. The Astros lost their first two games against the Brewers, while Chicago beat Cincinnati twice to end Houston's season.

The 2004 season got off to a delirious start in January when Houston native Roger Clemens signed a one-year contract to pitch for the Astros. He joined his best buddy, fellow Texan Andy Pettite, on a staff that already had Oswalt and Wade Miller, and the team and fans couldn't help but do some World Series dreaming in the middle of winter. Geoff Blum was traded to Tampa Bay for Brandon Backe, a move that was criticized at first but not for long.

The signing of Clemens electrified the Houston fans as nothing had since they signed Nolan Ryan—unless it was the day they lost him to the Rangers. Any acrimony that might have lingered from that debacle was smoothed over when Ryan signed a personal service contract with the Astros. Dierker was brought back to the broadcast booth later that season, and with a couple of the team's legends back in the fold, the Houston faithful settled in for what was sure to be a long and enjoyable season. It turned out to be the kind of season that could best be enjoyed after it was over, unless you could actually believe what happened at the end of the season while it was happening.

The team started off strong but soon began a struggle to stay above .500. Williams got most of the blame, and the popular notion was that McLane would wait to fire him until after the all-star game, which was being played at what was now called Minute Maid Park in Houston. That's what he did. By that time, Houston was in fifth place in the division, ten and a half games behind the Cardinals in the standings. Phil Garner was brought in to manage the team on an interim basis, but the team continued to struggle. There were, however, highlights of the milestone variety.

Clemens, who had an outstanding season and would win his seventh Cy Young Award at season's end, moved into second place on the all-time strikeout list behind Ryan, surpassing Steve Carlton in the process. Biggio got his 2,500th career hit. Those guys were on their way to the Hall of Fame, but the Astros looked nowhere near going to the playoffs.

Not content to simply fire the manager and hope for the best, McLane and general manager Gerry Hunsicker went after some more good players. One of the best was Carlos Beltran, and the Astros acquired him from Kansas City in exchange for Dotel. Lidge moved into Dotel's closer's spot and sparkled in that role. Still, on August 14, Houston was 56-60 and nineteen and a half games behind St. Louis and seven games behind Chicago in the wild card race.

Houston then got about as hot as any team can get and went 36-10 down the stretch, clinching the wild card spot on the last day of the season. By then, the Astros were practically unbeatable and, for the first time in their history, would not be an easy out in the playoffs either. Houston's first-round opponent was the Atlanta Braves, but this wasn't the same Atlanta team that had bumped the Astros rather unceremoniously out of postseason play in 1997, 1999 and 2001. Maddux and Glavine were gone to free agency, and John Smoltz was in the bullpen. The offense was powered by Chipper and Andruw Jones, along with Rafael Furcal and J.D. Drew. Nor was it the same Houston team. Bagwell, Biggio and Berkman were still there and would rise to the occasion in this year's playoffs, and Carlos Beltran was nothing short of sensational. The weak link for Houston was its pitching. Clemens and Oswalt offered the best one-two combination of starters in baseball, but the rest of the rotation was a hodgepodge of pitchers having mediocre years.

Opening on the road, Houston had to win at least one game in Atlanta to have much of a chance of advancing, and got it in game one, scoring four runs in the third inning and three more in the fifth as part of a 9–3 win. Bagwell and Raul Chavez went deep in game two, but Houston blew a two-run lead and lost in eleven innings, 4–2, on a two-run homer by Furcal.

Backe, a native of Galveston and a longtime Houston fan, got the call in game three. He knew well the fans' frustrations with the Braves, as he had shared in it as a fan, and he did his part to break the jinx, going six strong innings and allowing two runs. Morgan Ensberg took care of that with three RBIs, and Beltran added another homer to what would be a wildly impressive postseason for him.

Clemens took the mound in game four and was backed by five runs in the second inning, the big blow a three-run homer from Biggio. The Braves battled back against the Houston bullpen to tie it, and J.D. Drew drove home the game winner for a 6–5 win and a 2–2 tie in the series. It got worse from there. The Astros found out after the game that former teammate Ken Caminit had died at the age of forty-one, a sad end to a career and life that spiraled into drugs and madness after he left the team. The ghost of playoffs past was bad enough, but Caminit's death chilled veterans like Bagwell and Biggio, who were good friends with him.

Against that somber backdrop, Houston took the field in Atlanta for game five and put at least one of the ghosts to rest. Beltran homered twice, giving him four for the series, and drove in five runs in a 12–3 victory that gave Houston its first postseason series victory in team history. Bagwell and Biggio embraced on the field and in the dugout, the pull of conflicting emotions evident. They didn't need to say much. They knew what this win meant to them, to the Astros and to their long-suffering fans.

"We should all take pride in this," Bagwell said simply. "To beat an Atlanta team that has sent us home three times in the past and be able to play well, we should all take pride."

The Astros took that pride to St. Louis for their first-ever National League Championship Series. They also took Beltran, a source of pride for Houston almost from the time he first stepped off the plane in Houston that summer. He hit his fifth home run of the postseason in the first inning of game one in St. Louis, but the game turned into a slugfest. Teams with Albert Pujols on their side are going to win most slugfests, and this was a case in point as Pujols went deep twice in a 10–7 St. Louis win. Beltran homered again in game two, a 6–4 Houston loss that put the Cards up 2–0 in the series. In Houston for game three, Beltran homered yet again, and Clemens and Lidge shut Pujols and the Cardinals down for a 5–2 win that Houston simply had to have. For a team that spent most of the season with its back to the wall, facing another must-win in game five must have seemed only natural.

Game five was a classic. Backe turned in a performance for the ages, pitching eight innings of one-hit ball after retiring the first thirteen batters he faced. Woody Williams, a native of Houston, matched him by pitching seven innings of one-hit ball for the Cardinals. Beltran led off the ninth with a single and, with a one-two count on Berkman, stole second. The Cards decided to walk Berkman at that point, put the force on in the infield and take their chances with Jeff Kent, who homered to the left for Houston's first walk-off home run of the season and the most memorable in team history.

Houston had come back from nineteen and a half games out of first place in August to win the wild card and finally vanquished the Braves and won a playoff series. Down 0–2 in this series, the Astros had battled back to go up 3–2. From "dead in the water" in August, the term "team of destiny" was thrown out a few times as the series moved back to St. Louis. But Jim Edmonds homered for the Cardinals in the twelfth inning of game six to give the Cards a 6–4 win and force a deciding game seven, which the Cards won 5–2. The wait for a World Series in Houston, ground zero for baseball in the state since the sport's early days, would have to last at least another year.

"It's disappointing, no question about it," Bagwell said after the game when asked an obvious question. "They just beat us. There's nothing we can do about that. We battled the heck out of them. But as I've said, I'm proud as heck of this club. I will never forget this team. It's a heck of a bunch."

WORLD SERIES REALITY

The 2005 team was also a heck of a bunch, but it wasn't the same bunch by any means. The Astros offered Beltran more money than they had ever offered any other player, but he signed with the Mets. Nor did they sign Kent. Lance Berkman missed much of the early part of the season due to an offseason knee injury, and Bagwell stepped out of the lineup to have surgery on his arthritic right shoulder. The outfield was suddenly held down by a trio with mostly minor-league experience.

Clemens was once again one of the best pitchers in baseball, finishing with the league's lowest ERA (1.37), but was victimized by poor run support in several of his starts and went 13-8. Oswalt was dominating, winning twenty games for the second year in a row. Ensberg, Berkman and Biggio pulled much of the load offensively, but injuries and experience, along with the aging of the team's veterans, hit the Astros hard in the early going. This was, in many respects, a much different team than had come within one victory of a World Series berth the year before, but the Astros again performed a remarkable turnaround. After starting the season 15-30, Houston went 74-43 the rest of the way to once again claim a wild card berth in the postseason. Houston got the Braves again in the first round of the playoffs.

Pettite, back on the mound after missing most of 2004 with elbow troubles, got the win against the Braves in a 10–5 game one victory, but the Braves dropped Clemens and the Astros 7–1 in the second game. Houston battled back in the late innings in the next against the Atlanta bullpen for a 7–3 win and a 2–1 series edge, setting up what would be a marathon thriller in game four.

Atlanta used an Adam LaRouche grand slam as part of a 6–1 lead in that game, but a Berkman grand slam in the eighth brought Houston to within one. With two outs in the ninth, Ausmus lined a home run into the left-field seats to send the game into a whole bunch of extra innings. By the time it was over, after eighteen innings, a de facto double-header, Garner had used twenty-three players on his twenty-five-player roster, and Clemens was called on to pitch the final three innings on just two days' rest. Garner had no one else in the bullpen.

Finally, in the bottom of the eighteenth inning, rookie utility player Chris Burke connected against Joey Devine and drove the 553rd pitch of the game into the left-field seats, putting an end to the game and the series and setting up a rematch with St. Louis in the NLCS.

"I don't know how to explain it," Garner said. "It's been the darnedest thing I've ever seen. It looked like it was over. It looked like we were down and out. We came back. How do you explain that game? It's like the Sunday afternoon softball game where everybody on your block gets to play."

Another old foe, the St. Louis Cardinals, awaited Houston in the league championship series. The Cardinals had the best record in baseball and a lineup that made that fact easy to understand. Pujols was a terror at the plate, and they had a strong pitching staff anchored by Cy Young Award winner Chris Carpenter. Carpenter shut down the Astros in game one on five hits, but Houston rallied behind Oswalt for a 4–1 win in the second game. Houston got strong pitching performances from Clemens, Chad Qualls and Lidge and two RBIs from Lamb for a 4–2 win in game three.

Up 2–1 in the series against the team with the best record in baseball, Houston sat in the catbird seat when Backe and the bullpen shut down the Cardinals in game four.

Exactly forty-three years after Houston was awarded a Major League Baseball franchise, the Astros were one win away from going to their first-ever World Series, but the celebration had to wait after Pujols stunned the Astros and a sell-out crowd with a monstrous three-run shot in the ninth inning. If Houston was tight or bothered by its history of heartbreaking postseason losses, the team didn't show it on the plane ride back to St. Louis. One of Lidge's teammates looked out window of the plane and told Lidge, "Hey, Brad. There's the ball that Pujols hit."

Oswalt shut down the Cardinals in game five and got more than enough runs when Houston scored twice in the third inning on three hits, a sacrifice bunt by Oswalt and a wild pitch. Jason Lane homered in the fourth. A picture-perfect squeeze bunt by Adam Everett and an RBI

Albert Pujols launches a monster blast against Brad Lidge. *Harry Cabluck, Associated Press.*

single by Ensberg closed out the scoring, and Qualls and Dan Wheeler closed out the Cardinals.

For some in the Astros' clubhouse afterward, the game had special meaning because they knew all too well the team's tortured playoff history. Garner, in fact, was a member of the 1986 team that lost that classic series to the Mets.

"For us, forty-four years of getting close and not getting to the big dance has been frustrating," he said. "So this is a wonderful accomplishment for our city, for our organization, everybody that's been involved in it."

Biggio could hardly think of words to say. "It's unbelievable even to say the World Series and that we're going right now…It's a pretty emotional day."

The 2005 World Series between the Chicago White Sox and Houston Astros was called by *Sports Illustrated* "the most underwhelming World Series in history." The fans in Chicago would disagree wholeheartedly, and so would Houston fans, but only up to a point. Chicago, which had waited eighty-eight years for a World Series, swept the Astros, a franchise that had waited all of its forty-three years.

Chicago swept the Astros but did not blow them out, winning four games by a total of six runs. It had two game-winning home runs by two players—Scott Podsednik and Geoff Blum—who had hit one home run between them during the regular season. The White Sox won game four, 1–0, on a single, a sacrifice bunt, a groundout and an RBI single by series MVP Jermaine Dye.

Most underwhelming to the Astros was the fact that they had their chances. In game two, Andy Pettite pitched like the savvy playoff veteran he was and left a 4–2 lead for the bullpen to protect, which they did in no shape, form or fashion. Qualls gave up a grand slam in the seventh that made it 6–4. Pinch-hitter Jose Vizcaino drove in two runs for Houston with a double in the ninth, but Podsednik homered in the ninth for a 7–6 White Sox win.

On October 25, 2005, the first World Series game to be played on Texas soil was played at Minute Maid Park. Nolan Ryan threw out the first pitch. Given everything the team had overcome to get to this point, the Astros still thought they had a chance to win a World Series in dramatic fashion. Houston led 4–0 in the fifth, but the Sox got to Oswalt for five runs. Lane got him off the hook for the decision with a two-run double in the eighth. Houston left the bases loaded in the ninth and stranded six more in extra innings before Blum, a former Astro, homered to win it for Chicago in the fourteenth.

Backe pitched brilliantly in game four, going seven innings, scattering five hits, striking out seven and issuing no walks. Lidge was victimized for the Cardinals' lone and winning run in the ninth.

The disappointment in Houston was palatable but tempered with optimism. The team had shown that it was able to bounce back from diversity and plug in players from a strong minor-league system when necessary, but the team slowly disintegrated over the next five years and hasn't been in contention for a pennant since. Bagwell stayed on through the next season, but the bad shoulder wouldn't let him play. He finished with some astonishing numbers that have him in the top fifty all time in on-base percentage, slugging percentage, home runs and RBIs. Bill James ranks him as the fourth-best first baseman of all time.

Biggio played two more years, collecting his 3,000th hit in 2007. He retired after the '07 season with 3,060 hits and is one of just nine members of the 3,000-hit club to get all his hits with one club.

Fittingly, the Astros have retired both of their numbers.

A PERFECT MOMENT

Nolan Ryan was never one to simply ride off into the sunset. At his Hall of Fame induction ceremony, he said it took him two years to get over the fact that he was no longer in baseball. He remedied that by going back to work for the two Texas teams for which he had played so well and so long and by buying, along with son Reid and business partner Don Sanders, the Jackson, Mississippi team in the Double A Texas League and moving it to Round Rock.

That team, named by fans the Round Rock Express in honor of its owner, became one of the top-drawing franchises in Texas League history. As Ryan moved into the front office with the Texas Rangers, the Express, formerly an Astros farm team, switched its affiliation to the Rangers and moved to the Triple A Pacific Coast League. The Corpus Christi Hooks took Round Rock's place in the Texas League as the Astros Double A affiliate. As for Ryan, he was still trying to get the Rangers to the World Series. He joined the Rangers as team president in 2008.

The Rangers were still on a carousel that occasionally dipped quite low but never rose quite as high as expected. John Hart stepped down as general manager in October 2005, and twenty-eight-year-old assistant general manager Jon Daniels replaced him. Hanging on to good young players like Michael Young, Daniels set about rebuilding the team with a mix of youth and a sprinkling of veterans. He acquired Carlos Lee and Nelson Cruz from the Milwaukee Brewers. Sammy Sosa, originally drafted by the Rangers and who played his rookie year with the team (he hit his first major-

Longtime Oakland third base coach Ron Washington was hired to manage the Rangers in 2005.

league home run off Roger Clemens), was brought back long enough for him to hit his 600th career home run. Most significantly, Rangers manager Buck Showalter was let go, and Oakland third base coach Ron Washington was hired to take his place.

Washington was born in the Ninth Ward of New Orleans in 1952. The Kansas City Royals signed him in 1970, and he spent ten years in the minor leagues and knocked around the bigs for a few years with the Minnesota Twins, Orioles, Indians and Astros. He coached in Oakland for ten years, from 1996 to 2006, but he had never managed a game when the Rangers hired him at age fifty-four to take the reins of the Rangers.

For their part, the Rangers made a series of significant trades and acquisitions that gave Washington more to work with than what Showalter had. Determined to field a contender by 2010, the Rangers wheeled and dealed, losing slugger Mark Teixeira and top pitching prospect Jon Danks in the process, but they brought onboard players like Elvis Andrus, Neftali Feliz, David Murphy and others who would help make Daniels's vision come true.

During their rebuilding process, when the Rangers were good, they were very good, like in 2007, when they established a major-league record by scoring thirty runs against the Baltimore Orioles. That came three days after they struck out nineteen times against the Minnesota Twins.

The Rangers even acquired the number one pick of the draft in 2009, but it was the 1999 number one pick, the tremendously talented but deeply troubled Josh Hamilton. Injuries and a serious drug and alcohol problem derailed Hamilton's career before it ever got started. For two years, between 2004 and 2006, he was out of baseball completely. He battled his demons with rehab and a renewed commitment to his Christian faith and resurfaced with the Cincinnati Reds in 2007. The Reds traded him to Texas in 2008.

Off the field, the Rangers were a mess. In a time of financial crisis, owner Tom Hicks had his own money woes. He first offered to sell partial ownership and then a majority interest. In 2010, Hicks agreed to sell the team to a consortium that included—who else?—Nolan Ryan, but there were complications that delayed the sale and forced the Rangers to file for Chapter 11 bankruptcy. Much of the debt was in the form of salary, including some $25 million the team still owed Alex Rodriguez. It came down to a public auction with Ryan's group and a company

Josh Hamilton was a first-round pick in 1999, but it would be ten years before he became a star with Texas.

owned by Houston businessman Jim Crane, who had previously tried to buy the Astros. Ryan's group carried the day.

When he took over in 2004, Rangers general manager Jon Daniels had pegged 2010 as the year he expected the Rangers to seriously contend for an American League pennant. That prediction turned out to be right on the mark.

After a slow start, the Rangers caught fire in June, winning twenty-one games, including eleven in a row. There was no doubt that this team was going to be aggressive both on the field and in the front office. Nolan Ryan had been an aggressive pitcher, not afraid to come inside with some high heat. Ron Washington was an aggressive player, and as a third base coach in Oakland, he had made sure the Athletics played that way, too. He liked stretching singles into doubles and doubles into triples, and he was a proponent of stealing bases if they were there to be stolen. But there was a time just before the season began when there was some doubt whether Washington would manage the Rangers at all. Reports surfaced in March that he had tested positive for cocaine in 2009.

In an era when a lot of athletes will deny using drugs of any kind, even against overwhelming evidence to the contrary, Washington went to Ryan and Daniels and told them what had happened. He'd tried cocaine just a couple of weeks previously and got caught in a drug test. He offered to resign right then and there to save the team any further embarrassment. By the time the news became public, Ryan and Daniels had decided to give Washington another chance. When the story was published in *Sports Illustrated*, Washington owned up to it and apologized, promising to be a better man. Eventually, the story faded from the sports pages and talk shows.

The team wasn't exactly everything Ryan and Daniels wanted, so they got aggressive, too. They acquired former Cy Young Award–winner Cliff Lee

Ian Kinsler keyed the Rangers' drive to two American League pennants.

Michael Young played more than one thousand games with the Rangers before finally getting his shot in the postseason.

from the Seattle Mariners and catcher Bengie Molina from the Giants. They brought in Jorge Cantu, Cristian Guzman and Jeff Francouer to go along with all-stars Hamilton, Young, Kinsler, Elvin Andrus, Vladimir Guerrero and closer Neftali Feliz. The top of the starting rotation, with C.J. Wilson and Colby Lewis, was strong, but the Rangers needed a go-to guy if they expected to go very far in the playoffs. Lee was that guy.

The Rangers rolled to a 92-70 record and clinched the American League West pennant on September 25. Two days earlier, Michael Young had become the fourth Texas Ranger to play in at least 1,500 games without a postseason appearance for the Rangers.

The streak came to an end when the Rangers went to the Tropicana Field in St. Petersburg to play the Tampa Bay Devil Rays in the American League Division Series. Lee opened the series on the mound for the Rangers and was everything they had hoped he would be in just this situation. He struck out eleven and scattered five hits in a 5–1 Ranger victory, just their second playoff

C.J. Wilson was one of the young pitchers who helped Texas gain prominence in the American League.

win ever. In game two, C.J. Wilson shut down the Rays into the seventh inning, and the bullpen finished off the job; the big blow for the Rangers was a three-run home run by Young.

Back in Arlington, looking for their first-ever playoff win at home, the Rangers were up 2–1 in the seventh, but Tampa Bay scored five times in the final two innings for a 6–3 win. The Rays took back home field advantage the next night with a 5–2 win, sending the series back to Florida tied at two games apiece. To win the series, Texas would have to win again on the road.

An aggressive team all year, the Rangers didn't back off in the deciding game five. Andrus led off with a single, stole second and scored on a ground out by Hamilton. Tampa Bay pitcher David Price never suspected that Andrus would try something so reckless as trying to score from second on a ground ball, but he did. If the Rays thought that was an aberration, Cruz doubled in the fourth inning and stole third, scoring on catcher Kelly Shoppach's throwing error.

In the sixth, Guerrero did basically the same thing Andrus had done in the first, only he scored from second on another ground ball. This time, the Rays went for a double play, and Guerrero rounded third and headed for home, just in case. The throw to first was just a bit late, and Price waited for the call from the first base umpire before he threw home in an attempt to get Guerrero, who slid home just ahead of the tag. Kinsler hit a two-run home run for the Rangers in the ninth to seal the first playoff series victory in the Rangers' history. Until then, they were the only active team that had never won a playoff series.

Out of respect for Hamilton, the Rangers celebrated the milestone with ginger ale, holding off on the champagne until after he left. There was jubilation and celebration but also, this being the first round, anticipation. Their opponent in the American League Championship Series for the right to play in the World Series were the New York Yankees, who had played the Rangers ten times in the postseason and won nine times. Michael Young, for one, was ready.

"They're the defending champs," he said. "You've got to knock the champ off the mountain, and we're excited about the opportunity."

———

For one series, one game and one pitch—one moment in time in a game that is timeless and not determined by time—everything was perfect for the Texas Rangers and their fans, who had long suffered from the term "long-suffering" in reference to themselves. This time was going to be different.

With two outs in the ninth and the Rangers on the brink of vanquishing the ghosts of playoffs past and playing in the World Series for the first time in team history, Neftali Feliz was throwing smoke, fastball after fastball. With two strikes on Alex Rodriguez and a delirious home crowd hanging on every pitch, waiting for the celebration to begin, Feliz threw a slider that left A-Rod in that never-never land between swinging and bailing out. He did neither, taking a called third strike and signaling the start of a celebration like no other in Rangers' history.

A few minutes later, the legend, the Ryan Express, stood on the field, soaking it all in and trying to explain to reporters what it all meant. "The fans here have just waited a long, long time for this," he said. "Looking back to spring training, I just felt like this team was on a mission. There was a lot to overcome, but this is a resilient team, an unbelievably resilient team." He paused and looked up at the stands where fifty thousand people were in full celebration mode. "It's just…very, very rewarding."

Jim Reeves, writing the next day for ESPN Dallas.com, summed up the emotions of a longtime Ranger fans:

> One by one, the ghosts paraded by to pay their respects Friday night at Rangers Ballpark in Arlington. When there are 38 years of skeletons rattling around in the closet, that can take a while.

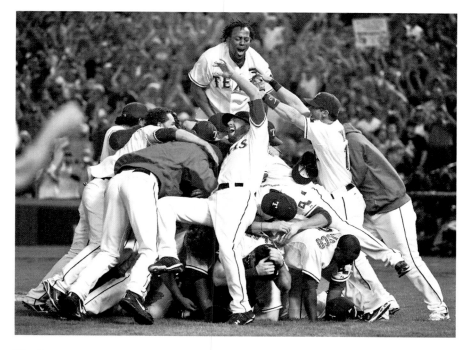

The Rangers celebrate after beating the New York Yankees for the AL crown. *Max Faulkner, Fort Worth Star-Telegram.*

Like wisps in the wind, all the old memories came flooding in, then faded away, vanquished perhaps forever: the 100-loss seasons those first two years in Texas; the David Clyde debacle; the four managers in one week; the Roger Moret catatonic trance; the armed guards on an off day at Arlington Stadium; the A-Rod promise that never materialized; even the bankruptcy that happened only yesterday.

They no longer matter. The Texas Rangers, finishing off the New York Yankees with a 6–1 KO punch in Game 6 of the American League Championship Series, are going to the World Series.

Of course, it's one thing to go to the World Series and quite another thing to win it. The Rangers didn't even come close to winning the series against the San Francisco Giants, who put together a motley assortment of rookies and "over the hill" veterans and journeymen to not only make it to the World Series but also win it. The series got off to a messy start in game one. A widely anticipated pitching duel between Lee and Tim Lincecum didn't work out that way as the Giants got to Lee for six earned runs and collected fourteen hits against Ranger pitching. Texas got eleven hits in the opener but committed four errors and lost 11–7.

That was the point where the Texas bats went silent, with hardly a peep heard the rest of the series. They scored just five runs over the remaining five games. They went eighteen and a third innings without scoring a run until Cruz popped a home run in the seventh inning of game five. Hamilton, the American League MVP, had just two hits, and Guerrero managed but one. The Giants' staff of Lincecum, rookie Madison Bumgarner (who threw a three-hit shutout in game three) and Matt Cain was superb. Nor was it a fluke. The Giants had the lowest ERA and the most strikeouts in the Majors in 2010, and they carried that into the series. Thirty-five-year-old Edgar Renteria was named the series MVP after his three-run home run in game five gave the Giants their first World Championship since 1954.

The only bright spot for the Rangers was game three, which they won 4–2 for the first victory in a World Series game by a Texas team.

The summer of 2011 was a record-setting one in Texas. The temperature hit one hundred degrees for the first time in May and stayed there every day for the better part of the summer. The record-setting heat was paired with a record-setting drought that would end up costing the state more than $5 billion in agriculture losses alone.

If the Rangers didn't stay exactly cool, they at least came across as calm and collected. They won a team record ninety-six games, and the unrelenting heat wave didn't keep the fans away, either. The Rangers drew 2,946,949 fans, breaking a record set in 1997. Nothing much ruffled this team. Lee signed with Philadelphia, but the Rangers' starting rotation, anchored by C.J. Wilson and Derek Holland, was solid all year long, as was Feliz in the closer's role.

Gurerro was also gone, but the Rangers signed all-star third baseman Adrian Belter to a six-year, $96 million deal that forced Young, somewhat reluctantly, into the role of designated hitter and utility infielder. Young had asked for a trade after the Rangers moved him to third to make room for Andrus, and he asked for a trade again this time. The two parties worked out their differences, and Young would again be a key contributor to the team's drive to a second-consecutive American League pennant, making the 2011 all-star team along with Hamilton, Wilson, pitcher Alexi Ogando and Adrian Beltre.

Curiously, in a summer marked by heat and drought, the Rangers had two games rained out. In May, a 7–0 Ranger lead that included a grand slam by Moreland, was wiped off the books when the game was canceled and rescheduled for July 7. At that game, Ranger fan Shannon Stone, a firefighter attending the game with his young son, fell to his death from the stands trying to catch a ball that Hamilton had flipped to him as he left the field. The tragedy cast a pall over the team and the stadium, and the Rangers continued to remember Stone and his family for the rest of the season.

The Rangers clinched their second-consecutive American League West title on September 23 following a 5–3 win over Seattle that made their magic number one. With the second-place Angels playing Oakland on the West Coast, the team and about twelve thousand fans stuck around the Rangers Ball Park in Arlington to watch the scoreboard as Oakland's 3–1 win over the Angels went final.

Drawing Tampa Bay again in the ALCS, the Rangers managed just two hits in the opener and lost 9–0, an unsettling reminder of the power shortage that had bedeviled them in the 2010 World Series. The Rangers rebounded the next day with a come-from-behind 8–6 win. In Florida for game three, Mike Napoli hit a two-run home run, and Hamilton drove in two more runs with a single, all in the fourth inning of a 4–3 win. The bats hadn't quite come alive, but they weren't somnolent either. One bat, the one belonging to Adrian Beltre, was seriously active in game four. Beltre belted three home runs, just the sixth major leaguer in history to hit three home runs in a single postseason game, joining such baseball luminaries as Babe Ruth, Reggie Jackson and George Brett. The Rangers needed every one of Beltre's bombs in another 4–3 win.

At a time when the Texas drought was making worldwide news, the Rangers' ALCS run against the Detroit Tigers was played between the raindrops. Game one had two hours of rain delays. Game two was rescheduled because of rain that never actually materialized, and the start of game four—in Detroit—was delayed two hours because of rain and went eleven innings. One person who didn't seem to mind was Cruz. He homered once in the soggy opener, a 3–2 Rangers win, and once they finally got around to playing game two, he hit two more home runs. The first one came in the seventh inning and tied the game at 3–3. The second one came in the ninth inning with the bases loaded and was the first walk-off grand slam in major-league postseason history; it made the Rangers 7–3 winners.

Cruz homered again in game four and also made a key defensive play when he threw a runner out at home on a deep fly ball to keep the game tied in the eighth. In the top of the eleventh, with the Rangers up a run, he smacked his fourth home run of the series in another 7–3 win.

The Tigers had won game three, and they won game five, 7–5, despite a two-run home run from Cruz. Detroit jumped to a 2–0 lead in game six, but the series essentially ended in the third inning when the Rangers scored nine runs. Young, mired in a slump through most of the

Nelson Cruz homered six times in the 2011 postseason.

series, doubled twice in the inning and drove in two runs each time. Cruz's sixth home run of the series, a major-league record for most home runs in a single postseason series, was the capper in a 15–5 Rangers win that punched their ticket to a second-straight World Series, this time against the St. Louis Cardinals.

Most fans, pundits and sportswriters expected a good series between two evenly matched teams, but no one predicted what lay in store.

How could they have?

THE BASEBALL GODS ARE FICKLE

A game of inches. People say that about a lot of sports, and they say it most often about baseball. Other games have some sort of time limit, but a baseball game, in theory, can last until the end of time. Until the last out is made, the game continues. Yogi Berra's classic line, "It ain't over until it's over" is funny because it's true. Never was it truer than in the 2011 World Series.

Exhibit A came in game one when St. Louis pinch-hitter Allen Craig looped a ball into right field that missed a sliding Cruz's outstretched glove by inches. In the ninth inning of game two, with the Rangers three outs away from going down 0–2 in the series, Ian Kinsler stole second on Cards' catcher Yadier Molina, whose rifle right arm and long string of disappointed would-be base stealers reminds people of Pudge Rodriguez in his prime. Molina had thrown out Kinsler when he tried to steal in game one, and the Rangers hadn't tried again, but this time Kinsler beat the throw by inches, or maybe millimeters. Andrus singled him to third and went to second when Pujols mishandled the throw from center field. Hamilton and Young drove in the game-tying and game-winning runs, respectively, on sacrifice flies.

Even a classic World Series, it seems, has to have one game that you throw out when rating it, and in this series that would be game three, a 16–7 Cardinals romp highlighted by three no-doubt-about-it home runs from Pujols. That trifecta put him in the company of Babe Ruth and Reggie Jackson as the only players to hit three home runs in a World Series game. As Cardinals manager Tony LaRussa said after the game, "That's pretty good company."

Military jets perform a flyover at the 2011 World Series.

Derek Holland overwhelmed the Cardinals with a two-hit gem in game four. Hamilton's RBI double would have been enough, but Napoli added a three-run home run for good measure to tie the series at two games apiece. The 4–2 Texas win in the fifth game was not a work of art—there were thirteen walks and three errors, and LaRussa, one of the shrewdest managers to ever pace a dugout, had trouble relaying his intentions from the dugout to the bullpen. In the end, Napoli's two-run double to right turned out to be the key blow in putting the Rangers up 3–2 heading into game six.

Ah, yes. Game six. This is the one that haunts Ranger fans and will for a long time. This was the one that got away more than once, one of the most tortuous losses in World Series history and one that cemented the 2011 World Series, and this game in particular, as one of the best ever. For most baseball fans and certainly for loyal Cardinal fans, it will be remembered as the most unlikely and dramatic comeback in history.

How many times did it look like the Rangers had the game and championship salted away? Two times? A dozen? More? But as mentioned earlier, baseball is played until the last out is made, and the last out in this game was a long time coming.

The Rangers were up 7–4 in the seventh inning after back-to-back home runs by Beltre and Cruz and an RBI single by Kinsler. The Cards got a run back in the eighth on a home run by Craig. Then, with two outs in the ninth, Berkman and Pujols on base and the Cards down to their last strike, David Freese caught up with a Feliz fastball and drove it deep into right field. Cruz might have made this catch in the familiar confines of the Rangers' Ballpark in Arlington, but in Busch Stadium he seemed a little unsure of where the fence was, and the ball fell in for a game-tying triple.

In the tenth inning, it seemed like maybe the baseball gods—and most fans believe in such deities—had perhaps ordained that ball to drop safely in order for Josh Hamilton to be the hero that Texas fans so desperately wanted him to be on this night. When Hamilton hit a two-run home run in the tenth, it seemed even better than a Hollywood ending. Sportswriters, columnists and talk show hosts all over the country scrambled to do justice to a storybook ending on baseball's biggest stage.

But the baseball gods are a fickle lot. In the bottom of the tenth, the Cards got one run on a groundout but were once again down to their last strike when Berkman, the Texas kid, hit a game-tying single. The Rangers and their fans believed in second chances, but how many chances are there in any given game or series?

Instead of Josh Hamilton, Freese was the hero of this game and the entire series. He was the storybook hero that the baseball gods ordained to take center stage. His home run to center field in the eleventh inning put an end to what *Sports Illustrated* writer Buster Olney (and others) called the greatest game in history. For the first time in nine years, the World Series would go to a game seven.

The Rangers jumped to a 2–0 lead in the first inning, but Freese, the Chosen One, tied it up in the bottom half of the inning with a two-run double. Craig homered in the third for a 3–2 Cardinals lead. It never got any better for the Rangers.

While fans and the media tried to find ways to describe the series and place it in a suitable historical context, fans were left simply hoping to find a reason to believe again. Maybe that reason had been there all along. Maybe Paul Burka, writing in *Texas Monthly* a month later, nailed the proper Texas perspective on what happened—and what did not happen—in the 2011 World Series. He wrote:

> *And yet, for the Rangers faithful, a more consoling lesson was there to be found—not in the narrow misses, but in the sight of team president Nolan*

Ryan, dressed impeccably in a suit, tie, and overcoat, watching grim-faced from the stands...Rangers fans should take heart in those images of Ryan, clenching his jaw as the game slid away, already planning, no doubt, his next few moves. If anyone can do battle with the merciless gods of baseball, it's him.

POSTSCRIPT

The Houston Astros opened their fiftieth year of existence in 2012 amid much change. After losing a team record 106 games in 2011, new Houston owner Jim Crane announced that the team will move to the American League West, in the same division as the Rangers, for 2013. Crane, who had previously tried to buy the Astros and who bid against Nolan Ryan for the Texas Rangers, also toyed with the idea of changing the team name. Reaction from fans and season ticket holders was swift and negative. In late January, Crane announced that he would do no such thing.

"You asked for change, and we added several fan-friendly initiatives last week, and we hope you like them," Crane said in a taped video message to season ticket holders. "We will continue to listen and look for additional ways to improve on and off the field.

"One thing we are not going to change is the name. We received strong feedback and consensus among season ticket holders and many fans, and we will not change the name Astros. The Houston Astros are here to stay."

The same can't be said of the Houston stars of the last few years. Roy Oswalt and Lance Berman were dealt away in 2010, and two of the Astros' most promising young players, Hunter Pence and Michael Bourne, were dealt in 2011. No one went into the 2012 season expecting the Astros to play or even contend for a World Series berth.

In Arlington, the Rangers signed twenty-five-year-old Japanese pitching star Yu Darvish to a six-year, $56 million contract. Team president Nolan Ryan said Darvish sincerely wants to be the best pitcher in baseball, and

Ryan for one thinks he has the tools to achieve that. That's a pretty heady recommendation for a player who has never thrown one major-league pitch. Manager Ron Washington signed a contract extension through 2014, as befits someone who has guided a team to the World Series two years in a row. The nucleus of the team that came within one strike—twice—of winning a World Series in 2011 returned for 2012 mostly intact.

The Texas League—long may it wave!—continues to add new teams and cities to its long and rich history, even as old teams fall aside or switch to other leagues. Last year, the Frisco Rough Riders were the league's top-drawing team, averaging better than 7,000 fans a game, and the Corpus Christi Hooks averaged better than 5,600.

Every year, cries of "Play ball!" and "Strike three!" and aspersions on the eyesight of certain umpires will be heard from the Rio Grande Valley to the Texas–New Mexico border and all points in between, from Little Leagues to the semipro leagues to the few who get paid to play the game. Lone Star diamonds shine brightly, and the dreams inspired by them live on.

Except for one. With the Astros rebuilding from a base of almost zero and bolting to the American League next year, it doesn't look like there will ever be an All-Texas World Series. If that were to happen in 2012, it would be the most incredible and unlikely turn of events in the long history of Texas baseball. And that's saying something.

BIBLIOGRAPHY

Alexander, Charles. *Our Game: An American Baseball History*. New York: Henry Holt and Company, 1991.

Angell, Roger. *The Summer Game*. New York: Viking Press, 1972.

Breslin, Jimmy. *Branch Rickey*. New York: Penguin Group, 2011.

Dewey, Donald, and Nicholas Acocella. *The Biographical History of Baseball*. New York: Carol and Graf Publishers, 1995.

Dierker, Larry. *This Ain't Brain Surgery: How to Win the Pennant without Losing Your Mind*. Lincoln: University of Nebraska Press, 2003.

Farmer, Neal. *Southwest Conference Baseball's Greatest Hits*. Austin, TX: Eakin Press, 1996.

Fink, Rob. *Playing in the Shadows: Texas and Negro League Baseball*. Lubbock: Texas Tech University Press, 2010.

Gay, Timothy. *Tris Speaker: The Rough and Tumble Life of a Baseball Legend*. Lincoln: University of Nebraska Press, 2005.

Guinn, Jeff, and Bobby Bragan. *When Panthers Roared: The Fort Worth Cats and Minor League Baseball*. Fort Worth: TCU Press, 1999.

Kahn, Roger. *The Boys of Summer*. New York: New American Library, 1973.

Kayser, Tom, and David King. *The Texas League's Greatest Hits: Baseball in the Lone Star State*. San Antonio: Trinity University Press, n.d.

Luke, Bob. *Willie Wells: "El Diablo" of the Negro Leagues*. Austin: University of Texas Press, 2007.

McKissack, Patricia C., and Frederick McKissack Jr. *Black Diamond: The Story of the Negro Baseball Leagues*. New York: Scholastic, Inc., 1994.

O'Neal, Bill. *The Texas League: A Century of Baseball.* Austin, TX: Eakin Press, 1987.

Reed, Robert. *Colt 45s: A Six-Gun Salute.* Houston, TX: Lone Star Books, 1999.

Rogers, Phil. *The Impossible Takes a Little Longer.* Dallas: Taylor Publishing Company, 1990.

Rogosin, Donn. *Invisible Men: Life in the Negro Baseball Leagues.* New York: Athenum Publishers, 1983.

Ryan, Nolan, with Jerry Jenkins. *Miracle Man: The Autobiography.* Dallas, TX: Word Publishing, 1992.

Seymour, Harold. *Baseball: The People's Game.* New York: Oxford University Press, 1990.

Shropshire, Mike. *Seasons in Hell.* New York: Donald I. Fine Books, 1996.

Stout, D.J. *Alpine Cowboys.* Austin: University of Texas Press, 2005.

Stowers, Carlton. *Oh Brother, How They Played the Game: The Story of Texas's Greatest All-Brothers Baseball Team.* Abilene, TX: State House Press, n.d.

Talmadge, Boston. *1939: Baseball's Tipping Point.* Albany, TX: Bright Sky Press, 2005.

Thorn, John, and Peter Palmer, eds. *Total Baseball.* 3rd ed. New York: HarperCollins Publishers, 1993.

MAGAZINES

Bamberger, Michael. "Hail to the Rajah." *Sports Illustrated* (June 24, 2002).

Beckham, Jeff. "Going Deep." *Texas Monthly* (November 2010).

———. "That Championship Season." *Texas Monthly* (November 2010).

Burka, Paul. "Strike Two." *Texas Monthly* (November 2011).

Chen, Albert. "Central Casting." *Sports Illustrated* (October 17, 2011).

Curtis, Bryan. "What Do You Think of the Rangers Now?" *Texas Monthly* (May 2011).

Dingus, Anne. "Rogers Hornsby." *Texas Monthly* (July 1988).

Habib, Daniel "Astronomical." *Sports Illustrated* (October 17, 2005).

Herskowitz, Mickey. "Little Joe: Rookie of the Year." *Baseball Digest* (September 1965).

Kurkjian, Tim. "Lone Star Fear." *Sports Illustrated* (April 9, 1995).

Lange, Marty. "Around the Horn: Rogers Hornsby Is a Baseball Star for the Ages." *Texas Highways* (August 2010).

Presswood, Mark. "Black Professional Baseball in Texas." *Texas Almanac* (2008–2009).

———. "The Minor Leagues in Texas." *Texas Almanac* (2008–2009).

Reiter, Ben. "The World Series Seeing Was Believing." *Sports Illustrated* (November 10, 2011).

Rushin, Steve. "Beeg and Bags Forever." *Sports Illustrated* (July 19, 2003).

———. "Home in the Dome." *Sports Illustrated* (August 16, 1994).

Verducci, Tom. "All for One." *Sports Illustrated* (November 7, 2005).

———. "Long, Strange Trip." *Sports Illustrated* (October 31, 2011).

———. "One of a Kind." *Sports Illustrated* (July 19, 1999).

Wilonsky, Robert. "A Bush League of Their Own." *Dallas Observer*, May 21, 1998.

Wolff, Alexander. "The Barrio Boys." *Sports Illustrated* (June 27, 2011).

WEBSITES

astrosdaily.com

baseball-almanac.com

baseball-reference.com

King, David. "Ross Youngs." thediamondangle.com.

ncaa.com/history/baseball/d1

texasrangers.mlb.com

Thompson, Bill. thompsonian.info/colts.

uiltexas.org/athletics/archives/baseball/tournament_record.html

INDEX

F

Falk, Bibb 26, 27, 59, 60
Farrell, Dick (Turk) 72, 73, 74, 75, 85
Fausett, Cy 51
Feeney, Chub 107
Feliz, Neftali 164, 167, 169, 177
Flood, Curt 92, 93
Ford, Ted 93
Forsch, Ken 103, 105
Fort Hood, TX 149
Fort Worth Cats (Panthers) 24, 30, 37, 53, 70
Foster, Andrew (Rube) 42, 43, 44, 48, 127, 151
Fox, Nellie 85
Franco, Julio 131
Freese, David 177
Frisch, Frankie 16

G

Galveston, TX 7, 112, 156
Garner, Phil 155, 160, 161
Garrido, Augie 128
Gay, Tim 21
Gehringer, Charlie 63
Glavine, Tom 141, 156
Gogolewski, Bill 97
Golden, Jim 72
Gomez, Lefty 91
Gonzalez, Juan 137, 139, 140, 142, 145
Gooden, Dwight 120, 121
Greer, Rusty 136, 137, 139
Grieve, Ben 130
Grieve, Tom 95, 113, 114, 117, 126, 130, 138
Griffey, Ken, Jr. 135
Griffin, Mike 55, 56
Guerrero, Vladimir 167, 168, 171
Guillen, Trini 59
Gustafson, Cliff 59, 60, 122, 123, 128
Guzman, Cristian 167

H

Hamilton, Josh 164, 167, 168, 169, 171, 172, 175, 176, 177
Hampton, Mike 142, 143, 144
Hand, Rich 93
Hargrove, Mike 99, 100
Harrah, Toby 95, 100
Hatcher, Billy 119, 121, 122, 125
Hatton, Grady 67, 86
Hays, Larry 128
Heist, Al 73
Herrera, William Carson (Nemo) 58, 59
Herzog, Whitey 95, 96, 98, 119
Hicks, Tom 151, 153, 165
Higgins, Pinky 37
Hitchcock, Sterling 143
Hofheinz, Roy 67, 83, 84, 85, 102
Holland, Derek 171, 176
Holquin, Lefty 59
Hooton, Burt 110, 123
Hornsby, Rogers 15, 21, 22, 23, 24, 35, 90, 151
Hoskins, Dave 52
House of David (baseball team) 37
House, Tom 123, 132
Houston Astros 74, 85, 98, 101, 110, 123, 161, 179
Houston Buffs (Buffaloes) 21, 28, 38, 53, 56, 66, 67
Houston Colt .45s 37, 71, 75
Houston Sports Association 67, 68, 78, 83
Houston, TX 7, 11, 21, 28–30, 37, 38, 41, 56, 66–74, 77–82, 84–86, 88–92, 96, 98, 99, 101–110, 118–123, 126, 128, 132, 138, 141–148, 154–162, 165, 179
Howard, Frank 91, 92
Howe, Art 103, 107, 132
Hubbard, TX 19, 20, 91
Hubert, Pat 57
Hunsicker, Gerry 140, 156
Hunter, Billy 100

Santo, Ron 67
Schiraldi, Calvin 122
Scott, Mike 118, 119, 120, 121, 125, 141
Sears, John (Ziggy) 32
Serena, Bill 64
Seymour, Harold 9
Shantz, Bobby 72, 73
Short, Bob 92, 95, 96, 97, 98, 100
Showalter, Buck 164
Shropshire, Mike 95
Sinton Eagles 55
Sisler, George 77, 91
Slaughter, Enos 67
Smith, Dave 110, 119, 120, 121
Smith, Hilton 48, 151
Smith, Levi 35, 36
Smith, Red 38
Smith, Tal 102, 140
Smoltz, John 141, 156
Sosa, Sammy 142, 163
Southwest Conference 25, 27, 60, 128
Spalding, Albert 9
Speaker, Tris 15, 19–22, 63, 91, 103, 142, 151
Spiers, Billy 142, 144
Stanky, Eddie 100
Staub, Rusty 86, 88, 89
St. Edward's University (Austin) 25
Steinbrenner, George 105
St. Louis Cardinals 11, 13, 22, 30, 38, 53, 92, 102, 160, 173
Stone, Mike 114, 126
Stoner, Lil 34
Strawberry, Darryl 120, 121
Strelzin, Paul 112
Sundberg, Jim 100
Sutton, Don 118

T

Tampa Bay Devil Rays 167
Teixeira, Mark 164
Temple, TX 28, 64
Terrell, TX 28
Texas League 11, 20, 24, 25, 28, 30, 34, 35, 37, 39, 52, 53, 55, 56,

63, 66, 67, 70, 74, 79, 111, 112, 163, 180
Texas Rangers 91, 93, 108, 113, 117, 123, 135, 151, 163, 169, 170, 179
Texon Oilers 35, 37, 55
Thon, Dickie 119
Toronto Blue Jays 123, 132
Traynor, Pie 38

U

University Interscholastic League (UIL) 58, 59, 128
University of Texas (Austin) 25, 35, 58, 59, 110, 122, 123, 127, 128
Unser, Al 108

V

Valentine, Bobby 113, 117, 123, 124, 126, 135
Virdon, Bill 77, 102, 107, 117, 141

W

Waddell, Rube 42
Wagner, Billy 142, 154
Wagner, Honus 22, 38
Walker, Harry (the Hat) 102
Walling, Denny 107, 110
Washington, Ron 164, 165, 166, 180
Washington Senators 31, 68, 91, 95, 113
Watchell, Paul 34
Watson, Bob 103, 104
Watson, Jim 74
Weaver, H.N. 30
Weiss, Walt 144
Wells, Willie 44–46, 51, 53, 126, 127, 149, 151
West Texas League 63
West Texas–New Mexico League 51, 63
White, Sol 43
Wichita Falls, TX 29, 39, 64
Williams, Bernie 140
Williams, Billy 67
Williams, Jimmy 153

ABOUT THE AUTHOR

Clay Coppedge has written for newspapers and magazines for more than thirty years, including fourteen as a sportswriter. He is currently a staff writer and columnist for *Country World* newspaper. Clay is also a columnist for TexasEscapes.com and a regular contributor to *Texas Co-op Power* magazine.